THE LABYRINTH OF NORTH AMERICAN IDENTITIES

THE LABYRINTH
OF NORTH AMERICAN
IDENTITIES PHILIP RESNICK

UNIVERSITY OF TORONTO PRESS

Poem extract on page 8:
Everwine, Peter (trans.). *Working the Song Fields: Poems of the Aztecs.* Spokane: Eastern Washington University Press, 2009. 43, 50. Reprinted by permission of Peter Everwine.

Poem extract on page 51:
Pacheco, Jose Emilio. *City of Memory and Other Poems.* Translated by Cynthia Steele and David Lauer. San Francisco: City Lights Books, 1997. English language translation copyright © 1997 by Cynthia Steele and David Lauer. Reprinted by permission of City Lights Books.

Poem extract on page 94:
Pratt, E.J. "Towards the Last Spike." In *Selected Poems.* Toronto: University of Toronto Press, 2000. 181–2. Reprinted by permission of the University of Toronto Press.

Library and Archives Canada Cataloguing in Publication

Resnick, Philip, 1944–
    The labyrinth of North American identities / Philip Resnick.

Includes bibliographical references and index.
Also issued in electronic format.
ISBN 978-1-4426-0552-7

    1. North America—Civilization. 2. Group identity—North America. 3. Transnationalism—Social aspects—North America. 4. National characteristics, American. 5. National characteristics, Canadian. 6. National characteristics, Mexican. I. Title.

E40.R48 2012   306.097   C2012-901177-0

We welcome comments and suggestions regarding any aspect of our publications—please feel free to contact us at news@utphighereducation.com or visit our Internet site at www.utppublishing.com.

North America
5201 Dufferin Street
North York, Ontario, Canada, M3H 5T8

2250 Military Road
Tonawanda, New York, USA, 14150

ORDERS PHONE: 1-800-565-9523
ORDERS FAX: 1-800-221-9985
ORDERS E-MAIL: utpbooks@utpress.utoronto.ca

UK, Ireland, and continental Europe
NBN International
Estover Road, Plymouth, PL6 7PY, UK
ORDERS PHONE: 44 (0) 1752 202301
ORDERS FAX: 44 (0) 1752 202333
ORDERS E-MAIL: enquiries@nbninternational.com

Every effort has been made to contact copyright holders; in the event of an error or omission, please notify the publisher.

This book is printed on paper containing 100% post-consumer fibre.

The University of Toronto Press acknowledges the financial support for its publishing activities of the Government of Canada through the Canada Book Fund.

Printed in Canada

Cover design by Pamela Woodland. Text design by Daiva Villa, Chris Rowat Design

RECYCLED
Paper made from recycled material
FSC
www.fsc.org   FSC® C103567

To the UBC library
and its invaluable staff and collections

Contents

"If I could start again, I would start with culture."
—Jean Monnet, on the construction of Europe

Acknowledgements

A version of Chapter 2 and the opening paragraphs of Chapter 9 were published as "New Worlds, New Jerusalems: Reflections on North American Identities," in the Mexican journal *Norteamérica*, Vol. 5, no. 1, (Jan.–June, 2010): 15–36. My thanks to Betsy Struthers for her skillful copyediting, to François Trahan for preparing the index, to Ashley Rayner for her editorial assistance, and to Michael Harrison for his ongoing support. My thanks as well to the three anonymous readers for the press and to Francisco Colom González for helpful comments on the manuscript.

Introduction

"There will come an age in the far-off years
when Ocean shall unloose the bond of things,
when the whole broad earth shall be revealed,
when Tethys shall disclose new worlds
and Thule not be the limit of the lands."
—*Seneca*, Medea[1]

W hat is North America? The question is not simply one of geographical location, physical characteristics, or political delineation. All these and more enter into any description of the continent that is the subject of this book. My interest, however, is in something that most studies of North America rarely embrace: the very idea of North America and the underlying question of whether a North American identity exists or is ever likely to come into existence.

North America is a vast continent, the third largest measured by size. At a minimum, it is composed of three continent- or semi-continent-sized states—Canada, the United States, and Mexico—straddling the Atlantic/ Caribbean on their eastern flanks and the Pacific on their western. Were the Caribbean and Central American states to be included in its geographical sphere—and for my purposes here I do not intend to do so—its contours would loom even larger.

Are there some deeper cultural characteristics or national patterns that bind together the three countries of this continent? Can we conceive of an allegorical figure of North America in the way that writers, artists, and weavers of myths have conceived of Europe, Asia, or Africa? Do tentative steps towards free trade agreements and more dramatic examples of population movement across national borders herald some sort of shared identity? And can a continent first peopled by indigenous populations, subsequently by Spanish, French, and British colonizers, then by a significant slave component from Africa and a veritable torrent of voluntary migrants from every corner of the world ever become the focus of something one could call North Americanness?

At first blush, one is tempted to say "No." In the pre-Columbian period, indigenous civilization in Mexico, for example, attained a level far superior to that of indigenous peoples in the present-day United States or Canada. And the continuing impact of those civilizations since the Conquest—and this despite the death by disease and exploitation of a large percentage of these indigenous people—has been much greater in Mexico than in the two other North American societies. Where colonization is concerned, the Spanish brought the values of a Catholic and ultimately counter-Reformation society with them; they imported a pattern of hierarchical rule that has prevailed through successive regimes since Mexico's achievement of independence in 1821. The United States was originally colonized by Britain; the nature of colonization varied among New England, the future mid-Atlantic states, Virginia, and the Carolinas; economic structures varied even more dramatically between north and south; and religious denominations were multiple. Yet the revolutionary break of the 13 Colonies in 1776 set in motion a series of events that were to make of the United States a substantially new civilization and dominant power not only in North America but in the world. As for Canada, New France laid the foundations for what was to become Quebec, with the British Conquest of 1759 sparking developments that would lead to Canadian Confederation in 1867 and all that has followed.

What could possibly be common to these three historical trajectories? One shared element—and here I build on the work of historians such as Herbert Bolton, J.H. Elliott, and Gérard Bouchard[2]—is the fact that all three were societies in the New World. The notion of "newness," of course, is strictly relative—in this instance to the Ptolemaic world that had encompassed Asia, Europe, and Africa but nothing beyond. Still, the impact of the discovery of what turned out to be neither India nor China but a whole new hemisphere— with two continents, as we now know, and not just one—was to be dramatic.

The discovery widened the geographical compass of the known world. It set in train a series of explorations and settlements that was to lead to the establishment of what today are 35 sovereign nation-states. It was to make the Atlantic the centre of trade involving four continents to the point where the Atlantic economy came to dominate the modern world for several centuries. It spawned a series of wars of independence, first the American, then various Latin American ones, giving impetus to both republican and democratic ideas. It allowed experimentation in religion while simultaneously providing the model of possible utopias for some who settled and others who dreamed of coming to America from some distant land. It engendered its own forms of exploitation, first of its indigenous people by European conquerors and settlers; subsequently of slaves imported from Africa to cultivate cotton, tobacco, and other crops in semi-tropical portions of the hemisphere; and in its industrial and commercial phases of significant sections of the immigrant working population that came to the Western Hemisphere.

The New World did not escape the cultural, political, or economic patterns of the Old. The languages that came to dominate were Old World languages—Spanish, Portuguese, French, and English, as the case might be—although with time each would take on New World characteristics. Christianity was the prevailing religion, in both its Catholic and Protestant guises, though here again syncretism and novelty often became the norm. Political practices were initially strongly influenced by metropolitan models, though innovation won through, particularly in countries such as the United States and Mexico that underwent wars for independence and revolutions. And if in the initial establishment of New World societies, economic power lay in Europe, New World resources—e.g., the bullion of Mexico and Peru and the staple products and eventually manufactures of the different colonies—came to play an important role in their own right.

Not only was the New World "new" in comparison to the Old, it was also new in the consciousness of its inhabitants, many of whom had crossed the ocean in their own lifetimes or were descended from those who had done so a generation or two before. The physical contours of the Americas differed greatly from those of Western Europe, with their turbulent rivers, extensive lakes, massive mountain ranges, and carpets of forests, with fauna and flora all their own.

Within the New World composed of the Western Hemisphere (Oceana would prove to be a new world somewhat apart), the crucial differences for long have been cultural ones. They have separated the Portuguese- and Spanish-speaking countries of Latin America from the predominantly English-speaking countries of North America above the Rio Grande. Much as the political and economic development of Spain and Portugal from the sixteenth century on came to differ significantly from that of Britain (and France), so did that of the United States and Canada differ from the countries to the south. Representative government, rule of law, subordination of the military to civilian authority, and elections with competing political parties as the basis of legitimacy were far more characteristic of the two northern North American countries. Levels of economic development as measured by criteria such as the GNP (gross national product) per capita have also been significantly higher in the two. So much has this been the case, at least until recently, that it has not been uncommon, especially in Canada, to think of North America exclusively in terms of Canada and the United States. In mirror fashion, for Mexicans and other Latin Americans the term *norteamericano* became a synonym for the United States, with Canada rarely entering into discussion.

It can be argued that the concept of North America as a locus of identity has loomed larger in recent decades as a direct consequence of the Canada-United States Free Trade Agreement of 1988 and the North American Free Trade Agreement (NAFTA) of 1994. For the first time, the three North American countries were bound by a single treaty limited to them alone. In a world where regional trade blocs have become the norm—the European Union, Mercosur (*Mercado Común del Sur*, involving South American states) and ASEAN (Association of Southeast Asian Nations)—this has been sufficient to spawn a mini-literature on North American integration.

Fair enough. But to the degree that there is or potentially may come to be a common North Americanness, it cannot be purely economically driven. Nor can it simply be something that like Athena springs out fully armed from the head of Zeus. It must have older roots, significantly deeper roots, than those spawned over the last couple of decades by free trade agreements.

This is what this book sets out to explore—not with the kind of encyclopedic range that a full historical treatment would require, nor with a swathe of data that a more statistically oriented social science approach might require. Mine will be a more eclectic approach, combining cultural, economic, historical, political, religious, and other characteristics in probing the underlying values of the three North American countries that are my subject of interest.

I have no hidden agenda, least of all any aspiration to some kind of North American political or economic union. *Tout au contraire.* I am fully aware of the enormous differences in power and influence between the

United States on the one hand and its two North American neighbours on the other. However, I am much more open to themes that crisscross obvious national lines and that may constitute the underlying material not of one single shared North American identity but of that labyrinth of North American identities that is the true subject of this study.

Notes

1 Seneca, *Tragedies*, *Medea*, trans. Frank J. Miller, Loeb Classical Library (Cambridge, MA: Harvard University Press, 1917), lines 376-79.
2 Lewis Hanke, ed., *Do the Americas Have a Common History? A Critique of the Bolton Thesis* (New York, NY: Knopf, 1964); J.H. Elliott, *Do the Americas Have a Common History?* (Providence, RI: John Carter Brown Library, 1996); Gérard Bouchard, *The Making of the Nations and Cultures of the New World* (Montreal, PQ: McGill-Queen's University Press, 2008).

Quetzalcoatl's Heirs

*"And so greatly did the Toltecs believe/in their priest Quetzalcoatl,
and so greatly obedient/and given to the things of their god
were they,/and so fearful of god,/that all obeyed him./All believed in
Quetzalcoatl/when he left Tula.../Suddenly he went towards the
center of the sea,/toward the land of black and red,/and there he
disappeared,/he, our prince Quetzalcoatl"*[1]

Where does myth end and reality take over? How can one do justice to the civilizations of indigenous peoples who populated North America before Columbus ever set sail to the New World? Does one simply take note of the wholesale extermination of vast numbers of indigenous people in the sixteenth century due to smallpox and other diseases, of their indentured status in Mexico for centuries thereafter, of their forced removal from the eastern and southern regions of the United States in the nineteenth century, of the development of a reserve system for indigenous peoples in Canada? What of the present status of North America's indigenous peoples and of the role they have come to play in the national mythologies of the three countries that make up the continent?

The archaeological remains of the Olmec, the Aztecs, the Mayas, and others total over 12,000 sites in Mexico.[2] Pyramids, sculptures, and legends of plumed serpents in the south and masks, totem poles, and headdresses in the north have left their marks on the collective memory not only of indigenous people but of those who came to displace them: "Teotihuacan is vast, its architecture monumental, and its deities vivid. It feels like the center of an empire when we walk within. This was a city-state, a true civilization."[3]

The geography of North America is dotted with indigenous names—
Mexico, Oaxaca, Sioux Falls, Dakota, Niagara, Canada. Indian words have
found their way into Spanish, French, and English. The intermingling of
peoples has wrought its own amalgams, nowhere more than in Mexico
where 70 per cent of the population is of mixed indigenous and European
origin—the *mestizaje*.

Yet there is no gainsaying the Conquest that began with Cortes and the
Aztecs in 1521 and resulted in a cascading series of defeats and expulsions
that reduced North America's indigenous peoples to a remnant of what
they once were. Politically, they were consigned to the role of a vanquished
people in all three countries. Economically, they were reduced to forced
labour in New Spain, pushed relentlessly westward and marginalized in
the United States, and reduced to a subordinate position through a series of
treaties with the Crown in Canada.

There is a paradox that arises over the place that Quetzalcoatl and the
indigenous peoples of the continent occupy in the larger North American
landscape. The civilizations that spawned the legends, temples, and monuments have crumbled into ruins. The indigenous peoples have experienced
little of the benefits of the new, European-derived civilizations that suc-
ceeded theirs. Yet their culture, or more correctly the culture of their ancestors, has at times been promoted by non-indigenous peoples to the highest
of planes.

José Vasconcelos, Mexico's Minister of Education in the early 1920s,
spoke of "slackening the cord that held Mexican art in abeyance to European,"[4] as he commissioned Diego Rivera, José Clemente Orozco, and others to paint their great murals of Mexico's indigenous past. For Orozco,
"the great American myth of Quetzalcoatl was a living one...pointing
clearly by its prophetic nature to the responsibility shared equally by the
two Americas of creating here an authentic New World civilization."[5] For
Carlos Fuentes, "the Indian world was a secret depository of all that we have
forgotten."[6] In similar fashion, one can point to James Fenimore Cooper's
nineteenth-century Leatherstocking novels, which romanticized the Indians of the American frontier, or to Henry Wadsworth Longfellow's long
elegiac poem, *The Song of Hiawatha,* which entered mainstream American
culture almost on the day it appeared in 1855: "I saw the remnants of our
people/Sweeping westward, wild and woful,/Like the cloud-rack of a
tempest,/Like the withered leaves of Autumn."[7] One can highlight the role
that First Nations lore played in the opening ceremonies of the Vancouver

Winter Olympics of 2010 and in the adoption of an Inuit cairn named Ilanaq as the Games' logo. Indigenous myths loom large in the cultural perceptions of the non-indigenous peoples that constitute North America today.

Who are Quezalcoatl's true heirs? Are they the indigenous peoples of Mexico, who constitute some 10 per cent of the country's population and at the same time are the most marginalized sectors of Mexican society? The 1 per cent to 2 per cent of the populations of the United States or Canada who can claim native ancestry and who have been forced to integrate into those societies on terms largely set by their non-indigenous majorities? Those of mixed background, for whom the plaque in the Square of the Three Cultures at the centre of Mexico City reads: "On August 13, 1521, heroically defended by Cuauhtemoc, Tlatelolco fell into the hands of Hernan Cortes. It was neither a triumph nor a defeat: it was the painful birth of the mestizo nation that is Mexico today." Or the larger populations of all three North American societies, who in their own strange ways see themselves as fulfilling Quetzalcoatl's parting prophecy?

In a sense, the answer is all of the above. There are many indigenous pasts. Countless indigenous tribes have disappeared, their oral histories entering the realm of a spirit world with only distant echoes reverberating today. For others, the past remains alive in the consciousness and customs of ancestors who survived warfare and conquest, indentured labour and horrific disease. In New Spain, for example, it is estimated that 12.5 to 25 million Indians perished from disease in the century after 1519, leaving barely 10 per cent of the indigenous population extant.[8] Others perished in failed rebellions by the Yaquis, Yopes, Tarahumara, Tzeltal, Seri, and Maya between the sixteenth and eighteenth centuries. They took part in the struggles against the Spanish at the time of Mexican independence but got no reward in the political system that emerged.[9] They were given formal recognition as tribes, but little more, through Article 2 of the Mexican Constitution of 1917.[10] Greater recognition in the 1920s and 1930s came from artists and intellectuals and with the agrarian reforms of the Cárdenas period, which transferred lands to collectively owned farms, called *ejidos,* many of them with indigenous populations. Sadly, their economic viability turned out to be severely limited, and the postwar economic boom passed by indigenous people.

Nor did any substantial change result from the Zapatista Rebellion in Chiapas in 1994 or the still-born St. Andres Accords of 1996 between the Zapatistas and the Mexican government, which would have provided for autonomous indigenous communities. The current status of indigenous people in Mexico continues to be equated with extreme poverty with a lack of potable water, sewage, plumbing, electricity, and basic health or education services. Symbolically, they remain at the bottom of the heap. One small illustration of this is the mistaking of Topilitzin, the indigenous star of the film *The Other Conquest,* for the film director's chauffeur when the two showed up for an interview at the studio of *Televisa* (the largest mass media conglomerate in Latin America) and this despite Topilitzin's face appearing on huge billboards everywhere.[11] And politically, Mexico, like other Latin American countries, is unwilling to contemplate any form of domestic sovereignty for its indigenous peoples. "Until the Mayan rebellion of Chiapas in 1994, the issue of indigenous people's sovereignty was unspeakable in Latin America.... Following a strict Napoleonic tradition, in Latin America the notion of sovereignty is applied exclusively to the nation-state."[12]

The indigenous peoples of the United States from the time of King Philip's War in Massachusetts in the early eighteenth century found themselves at the losing end of a struggle for survival. There was little sympathy for the Cherokees and others deported from the east or the south in the aftermath of the immensely popular Indian Removal Act of 1830 nor for those who were persecuted in the repeated Indian Wars from the Dakotas in 1862 to the Great Sioux War of 1876–77. As one Minnesotan settler put it bluntly, "So far as I am concerned, if they [the Dakotan Indians] are hungry, let them eat grass or their own dung."[13] As a Sioux witness to the massacre of his people recalled, "The snow drifted deep in the crooked gulch, and it was one long grave of butchered women and children and babies, who had never done any harm and were only trying to run away."[14]

Have things changed for the better in the ensuing century and a half? Not overwhelmingly. The most notable legislative improvement came with the Indian Reorganization Bill of 1934 with provisions to "conserve and develop Indian lands and resources, extend to Indians the right to form business, to establish a credit system for Indians, and to grant certain rights of home rule to Indians."[15] There was the Red Power movement that briefly flared in the late 1960s and early 1970s only to fade away. There has been some development of reserve-based capitalism, particularly in the gambling industry. But hard realities do not change quickly. As a recent United Nations report pointed out, "In the United States, a Native American is 600 times more likely to contract tuberculosis and 62 per cent more likely to commit suicide than the general population."[16]

Canada may be slightly ahead of the United States and Mexico with regards to recognition and treatment of its indigenous population, but only modestly so. The Indian Act, through its various iterations, has made Aboriginal peoples subjects of the Crown. The residential school system, which tore First Nations children away from their biological families and indigenous communities for long stretches of time, significantly eroded their cultural roots. Proposals for wholesale political change—e.g., constitutionalized recognition of forms of self-government contained in the Charlottetown Accord of 1992 and various recommendations of the Royal Commission on Aboriginal Peoples for nation-to-nation relationships between First Nations and other Canadians—proved stillborn. The median income for Aboriginal people in Canada in 2006 was $18,962 as compared to $27,097 for other Canadians.[17] Problems of alcoholism, drug dependency, suicide, incest, and water purity are rampant on reserves; nor are the conditions of urban Aboriginal peoples a source of national pride.

The direct heirs of Quetzalcoatl are still awaiting his return, which, like that of the Second Coming, seems to be on indefinite hold.

What about the mestizo theme, so prevalent in Mexican political discourse and with more limited sway in the two countries to the north? Concubinage and racial mixing were symbolized in the union between Cortez and Malinche, his Aztec interpreter and mistress; further north in Virginia, between Pocahontas, daughter of an Indian chief, and John Rolfe, a Jamestown colonist; and still further north between Baron de Saint-Castin, a member of the Carignan-Salières regiment in Quebec, and an Aboriginal woman named Marie-Mathilde Madokawando.[18] A majority of Mexicans today claim mestizo background, but political and economic power still remains highly concentrated in the hands of lighter-skinned descendants of Spanish and other European settlers.

Much like caste differences in India, gradations of skin colour weigh heavily in Mexico. This is the exact opposite of what Vasconcelos professed in the 1920s with his notion of a single cosmic race: "It is in the fusion of ethnic stocks that we should look for the fundamental characteristics of Ibero-American idiosyncrasy…we in America shall arrive, before any other part of the world, at the creation of a new race fashioned out of the treasures of previous ones: the final race, the cosmic race."[19] In practice, the terms of ethnic integration were set by those of European background, and the playing field was not one on which those of mixed background could prevail. The mestizo idea has served Mexico well mainly at the level of national myth-making.[20]

Perhaps the most telling part of Quetzalcoatl's legacy, ironically enough, lies with the larger populations of all three North American states. They are the custodians of lands once occupied by indigenous peoples, of their resources, their by-ways, and their archaeological remains. In an odd kind of way, they have appropriated their footprints as a feature of their own historical narratives.

A perfect example of this is Frederick Jackson Turner's 1893 thesis about the western frontier of the United States:

> The wilderness masters the colonist. It finds him a European in dress, industries, modes of travel, and thought. It takes him from the railroad car and puts him in the birch canoe. It strips off the garments of civilization and arrays him in the hunting shirt and the moccasin. It puts him in the log cabin of the Cherokee and Iroquois and runs an Indian palisade around him. Before long he has gone to planting Indian corn and plowing with a sharp stick; he shouts the war cry and takes scalp in orthodox Indian fashion. In short, at the frontier the environment is at first too strong for the man. He must accept the conditions which it furnishes, or perish, and so he fits himself into the Indian clearings and follows the Indian trails. Little by little he transforms the wilderness, but the outcome is not the old European.... The fact is, that here is a new product that is American.[21]

For a Canadian example, one can point to Harold Innis's observations about the impact of the fur trade and the old Aboriginal travel routes on the contours of the subsequent Canadian economy: "'The lords of the lakes and forests have passed away' but their work will endure in the boundaries of the Dominion of Canada and in Canadian institutional life.... We have not yet realized that the Indian and his culture were fundamental to the growth of Canadian institutions."[22] In the Mexican case, Octavio Paz made the following claim in his Nobel Prize lecture of 1990: "The temples and gods of pre-Columbian Mexico are a pile of ruins, but the spirit that breathed life into that world has not disappeared; it speaks to us in the hermetic language of myth, legend, forms of social coexistence, popular art, customs. Being a Mexican writer means listening to the voice of that present, that presence. Listening to it, speaking with it, deciphering it: expressing it."[23] Footprints and legends of the past percolate through to those who have come to populate lands where pre-Columbian peoples once prevailed.

The myth of Quetzalcoatl, the plumed serpent, like that of other indigenous legends, retains a fascination across the ages, ethnic and racial lines. As Jacques Lafaye has noted in the Mexican case, "If the myth of Quetzalcoatl has retained its vitality throughout its successive avatars, in colonial and independent Mexico alike, it is because he is the symbolic expression of the colonial past…the new incarnation of the Indian messiah from the depths of the ages, a Phoenix with each new 'sun' from the ashes of the preceding sun."[24] Indigenous peoples become Quetzalcoatl—expelled, humiliated, and dispossessed. At the mythic level, however, their legends are appropriated by successor civilizations, lending them an authenticity as New World ones. The return of Quetzalcoatl does not occur in the way that the legends suggest but as new civilizations that have been built on the geographical territories of the old.

Does that give those who have displaced the indigenous peoples who first populated the continent some kind of proprietary claim to their legends and lore? Of course not. The new civilizations—European in origin—bear little resemblance to the ones that prevailed before the coming of Columbus. Nor can they be said to have been built upon their foundations—though the survival of the early settlers and their ability to adapt to their new habitat would have been much impeded without the help of indigenous peoples.[25]

What is involved is something more symbolic or sinister, depending on one's point of view—an elective affinity for myths and names, which help to give a New World rootedness to these post-Conquest civilizations. If one asks what makes Canada, the United States, and Mexico uniquely North American, geography is one part of the story. But so too are the indigenous civilizations that have left major archaeological sites, artistic traditions, and spiritual lore to which the non-indigenous populations of the three countries of this continent can relate. In doing so, they define themselves as North American in a way that their ancestors—first generation or tenth—in the Old World cannot.

They also touch something of the quest for the universal that characterizes civilizations old and new. Mexico's outstanding archaeological ruins have been compared with those of Assyria or Egypt in terms of their place in world culture.[26] Some have evoked the ruins of Rome or Athens when viewing Mount Albán, high on a mountaintop against the blue Mesoamerican sky of Oaxaca.[27] And if one is looking for even deeper metaphysical soundings, who could not be moved by some of the poems that have come down to us from the pre-Columbian period?

I cry out because death
lays waste our work, with death
the song breaks off,
We have so little time to look at the earth.
. . .

All of us go, all of us!
Nobody lasts on earth,
and who can tell us
if we ask: where shall we look
for our friends?[28]

So it is in the realm of myth that the indigenous lore of the past continues to haunt the North American continent of today. Quetzalcoatl has become Janus-faced, one face incarnating an indigenous past, the other the post-Conquest civilizations that have arisen in its place. This part of his legacy represents a return of the suppressed in a displaced and subordinate form that bears only passing reference to the real world of indigenous peoples today.

And what about these modern indigenous peoples? At best, "they have doggedly fought to survive as distinct societies in the land of their ancestors...forcing non-Native Canadians to redefine their concept of Canada. This is probably best symbolized by the recent public acceptance of the idea that Aboriginal people were Canada's 'First Nations.'"[29] At worst, they have been shamefully treated, their legends appropriated, with poverty their continuing lot. They have been marginalized in the American context, their presence more celebrated in the names of athletic teams than in mainstream American life. As for Mexico, "Proud of its Indian past, [it] seems ashamed of its Indian present. Government buildings are covered with murals and sculptures extolling the heroism of the Aztecs, while museums house the exquisite jewellery, pottery and artifacts found in pre-Hispanic ruins. But the Indians themselves, the direct descendants of that 'glorious past,' remain a conquered race, victims of the worst poverty and discrimination to be found in Mexico today."[30]

Such are the hidden and contradictory veins of North American identity.

Notes

1 Miguel Leon-Portilla, *The Ancient Mexicans through their Stories and Songs* (Mexico: Fondo de Cultura, 1961), 37.

2   Leon-Portilla, *The Ancient Mexicans*, 33.

3   Neil Baldwin, *Legends of the Plumed Serpent: Biography of a Mexican God* (New York: Public Affairs, 1998), 26.

4   Baldwin, *Legends of the Plumed Serpent*, 145.

5   Baldwin, *Legends of the Plumed Serpent*, 153.

6   Carlos Fuentes, *A New Time for Mexico* (New York: Farrar, Straus and Giroux, 1996), 201.

7   Henry Wadsworth Longfellow, *Hiawatha, a poem,* chap. XX1, Electronic Text Center, University of Virginia Library, http://etext.lib.virginia.edu/toc/modeng/public/LonHiaw.html, accessed May 22, 2011.

8   John Ross, *El Monstruo: Dread and Redemption in Mexico City* (New York: Nation Books, 2009), 43–44.

9   Eric van Young, *The Other Rebellion: Popular Violence, Ideology, and the Mexican Struggle for Independence, 1810–1821* (Stanford: Stanford University Press, 2001).

10 "The Mexican nation is unique and indivisible. The nation is pluricultural based originally on its indigenous tribes which are those that are descendants of the people that live in the current territory of the country at the beginning of the colonization and that preserve their own social, economic, cultural, political institutions. The awareness of their indigenous identity should be fundamental criteria to determine to whom the dispositions over indigenous tribes are applied. They are integral communities of an indigenous tribe those that form a social, economic, and cultural organization." Mexican Constitution, 1917, article 2.

11 Salvador Carrasco, "The Invisible Sight," in *The Zapatista Reader*, ed. Tom Hayden (New York: Nation Books, 2002), 173.

12 Stefano Varese, *Witness to Sovereignty: Essays on the Indian Movement in Latin America* (Copenhagen: Danish Ministry for Foreign Affairs, International Work Group for Indigenous Affairs, 2006), 284.

13 Clarissa W. Confer, *Daily Life during the Indian Wars* (Santa Barbara: Greenwood, 2011), 116.

14 John Gapper, review of *American Colossus: The Triumph of Capitalism, 1865–1900*, by H.W. Brands, *Financial Times*, December 17, 2010: 10.

15 Robert Berkhofer Jr., *The White Man's Indian* (New York: Vintage, 1979), 184.

16 *Guardian Weekly*, "First Americans Come Last," January 29, 2010: 25-27.

17 Canadian Centre for Policy Alternatives study, cited in *Globe and Mail*, April 8, 2010: 4.

18 David Hackett Fischer, *Champlain's Dream* (New York: Simon and Schuster, 2008), 509.

19   José Vasconcelos, *The Cosmic Race* (Baltimore: Johns Hopkins University Press, 1997), 19, 40.

20   For a critique of Vasconcelos's construct, see Luis A. Marentes, *José Vasconcelos and the Writing of the Mexican Revolution* (New York: Twayne, 2000), 80, 103; Marilyn Grace Miller, *Rise and Fall of the Cosmic Race: The Cult of Mestizaje in Latin America* (Austin: University of Texas Press, 2004).

21   Frederick Jackson Turner, "The Significance of the Frontier in American History," 1893, http://www.learner.org/workshops/primarysources/corporations/docs/turner/.html, accessed December 22, 2011.

22   Harold Innis, *The Fur Trade in Canada*, rev. ed. (Toronto: University of Toronto Press, 1970), 392.

23   Octavio Paz, Nobel Prize Lecture 1990, http://nobelprize.org/nobel_prizes/literature/laureates/1990/paz-lecture.html, accessed December 22, 2011.

24   Jacques Lafaye, *Quetzalcoatl and Guadalupe: The Formation of Mexican National Consciousness 1531–1813* (Chicago: University of Chicago Press, 1987), 13.

25   Fischer, *Champlain's Dream,* 510.

26   German Arciniegas, *Latin America: A Cultural History* (New York: Knopf, 1966).

27   Oliver Sacks, *Oaxaca Journal* (Washington, DC: National Geographic, 2002), 125.

28   Peter Everwine, trans., *Working the Song Fields: Poems of the Aztecs* (Spokane: Eastern Washington University Press, 2009), 43, 50.

29   Arthur Ray, *An Illustrated History of Canada's Native People* (Toronto: Key Porter, 2010), 398.

30   Alan Riding, *Mexico: Inside the Volcano* (London: Tauris, 1987), 20.

TWO

Chosen Peoples

"The Lord shall have made his American Israel high above all nations."

—*Ezra Stiles*[1]

The religious strand was of particular importance in legitimizing the concept of a New World and of the Christian-rooted societies—both Catholic and Protestant—that were to emerge there. From the beginning, the Spaniards saw themselves as God's chosen people:

> That Columbus assumed the Second Coming of Christ is indicated in The Book of the Prophecies which he wrote shortly before his last voyage to America.... It amplified a statement which he had made to the former nurse of Prince John: "God made me the messenger of the new heaven and the new earth." In his book he wrote that the blessed event was to be preceded by the opening of the New World, the conversion of the heathen, and the destruction of Antichrist, or Satan.... The Spanish were to be the chosen people, successors to the children of Israel.[2]

For some, Mexico was a new Jerusalem, with Catholicism a crucial component of the consolidation of the Spanish Empire and of the governance of New Spain (i.e., Mexico). "The conquest of America was like a new departure of the youthful forces of Europe on a new crusade, this time to the West. It was as if, having failed to reconquer and retain the historical Jerusalem, the nephews of the Crusaders had departed to build a New Jerusalem at the antipodes of the Old."[3]

Equally important in the Mexican context was a fusion of earlier beliefs with Christian, as in the powerful vision of the Virgin of Guadalupe, who according to legend was first sighted in 1531 by an indigenous herdsman, Juan Diego, shortly after the Spanish Conquest and who was destined to play a recurrent role in the subsequent history of Mexico from the Independence struggle of the 1810s, to the Zapatistas of the 1910s, to the anti-revolutionary *Cristeros* movement of the 1920s, to the canonization of Juan Diego by Pope John Paul II in 2002. Father Florencia, a seventeenth-century Mexican cleric, cited Psalm 147 in support of the emerging cult of Guadalupe: "He has not done the like for any other nation."[4] A sermon by the Jesuit preacher, Juan de Goicoechea, in 1709 at Tepeyac, the site of the Virgin's sanctuary just north of Mexico City, stated that "the Virgin wished to be an *Indiana*...to take up residence in this 'New Jerusalem, New Spain.'"[5] For Ignacio Manuel Altamirano, a late nineteenth-century liberal novelist and journalist, "The day in which the Virgin of Tepeyac is not adored in this land, it is certain that there shall have disappeared, not only Mexican nationality, but also the very meaning of the dwellers of Mexico of today."[6]

There was also room in the religious/mythic mindscape of Mexico for the re-appropriation of pre-Christian divinities, the most important of which was Quetzalcoatl, the vanished (and vanquished) figure of Olmec and Aztec lore referred to in the previous chapter. Catholicism acquired a syncretic character in Mexico, as "the myth and worship of the local Virgin Mary became the hub of a Creole Catholicism which presided over a large Mexicanization of Christianity by translating sundry Indian myths into the Roman rite."[7] In much the same way, "The Mexican Days of the Dead involve a complex mixture of Christian and pagan ideas. The dead are believed to return and their return is a mixture of joy, satire and grief."[8]

Catholicism has played a dominant role in Mexico from the post-Conquest period down to the early twentieth century. Its economic importance extended to Church control of banking, credit, and much of the rental property in the capital by the mid-1700s.[9] Its seminaries were the main organ of Mexican education from colonial times until the late nineteenth century, with priests the directors of the people's conscience, for good or ill.[10]

Although two priests, Miguel Hidalgo and José María Morelos, played a leading role in the Independence movement of the 1810s, the Church as a whole was strongly opposed.[11] As Daniel Cosío Villegas argued, "Mexico achieved its independence under the worst historical conditions. The long struggle to attain it destroyed part of the national wealth; another part, persecuted, fled to Spain; and the major part of what was left belonged to the Catholic Church, enemy of the new nation."[12] The Church tended to support the most conservative elements in Mexico over the next century, including Porfirio Díaz during his long dictatorial rule.

This helps explain the violent anti-clericalism that came to characterize Mexico at the time of the Revolution, not unlike what France had experienced during its own. According to Pancho Villa, one of the legendary figures of the Revolution, "We Mexicans have suffered the Spanish for 300 years…. They introduced among us the greatest superstition the world has ever known: the Catholic religion. This alone is more than enough reason to kill them."[13] Francisco Múgica, the drafter of Article 3 of the 1917 Constitution with its strongly anti-clerical provisions, stated, "I am an enemy of the clergy because I consider it the most baneful and perverse enemy of our country."[14]

On the other side, one can point to persistent clerical influences in postrevolutionary Mexican society. Conservative forces, opposed to the secularization of Mexican education in the 1920s and to the limitations on public expressions of Catholicism, organized their opposition in the *Cristero* movement, which had strong support in the western part of the country.[15] In 1941, Marcial Maciel founded the ultra-conservative Legionaries of Christ, preaching unquestioned obedience to superiors. According to one account, "Maciel's early associates included Miguel Alemán, Mexico's president from 1946–52 and the creator of his country's tourist industry, and went on to include his compatriot Carlos Slim, the world's richest man…. He was also close to the Garza-Sada family in Mexico, which controls a billion-dollar empire based in the northern Mexican industrial metropolis of Monterrey…. In the world of the arts, his contacts included Placido Domingo, the Spanish tenor who grew up in Mexico, and Mel Gibson, the actor and director."[16] Mexican religious fervour was exemplified during five papal visits to Mexico between 1979 and 2002, and public expressions of faith became a hallmark of presidents such as Vincente Fox and Felipe Calderón.

Nonetheless, religious pluralism has been more characteristic in modern times. Whereas 98 per cent of the Mexican population was Catholic in 1950, the percentage had fallen to 88 per cent by 2000. There is a stronger evangelical Protestant presence than before, along with non-religious spiritualism, such as the ecological movement. Secularism has a strong presence in Mexico City, where both abortion and gay marriage have been legalized. The Mexican reality today is not unlike that of many other Western societies, with religion no longer as dominant as before.[17]

For the Puritans coming to New England, America was the New Jerusalem and, for its early settlers, the fulfillment of the Kingdom of God on earth. Religious ideals that had been suppressed in the Old World prospered in the New. John Winthrop, on the voyage of the *Arabella* in 1630, hailed New England as the "Citty upon a Hill, the eies of all people are upon us."[18] Increase Mather, in a sermon in 1674, *The Day of Trouble is Near,* thundered, "here the Lord have caused as it were New Jerusalem to come down from Heaven. He dwells in this place[,] therefore we may conclude he will scourge us for our backslidings."[19] John Edwards, the figure associated with the eighteenth-century Great Awakening, prophesied in a sermon entitled *The Latter-Day Glory is Probably to Begin in America,* "There are several things that seem to me to argue that the sun of righteousness, the sun of the new heavens and the new earth, when he rises…shall rise in the west, contrary to the course of things in the old heavens and earth.… The sun of righteousness has long been going down from east to west; and probably when the time comes of the church's deliverance from her enemies, the light will shine in the west, till it shines through the world like the sun in its meridian brightness."[20]

The implications of religious faith for the United States have been legion. The idea of a covenant, rooted in Calvinism, opened the door to the notion of consent of the governed.[21] Competition among religious sects may well have sown the seeds for the pluralist nature of American democracy in contrast to the more hierarchically organized societies in Latin America with their established clergies.[22] The veneration for American nature could itself become a projection of religious sentiment.[23] American nationalism has often taken on a chiliastic or eschatological hue, embodying a Christian interpretation of the sacred.[24] American Christianity has tended to take the notion of God's kingdom on earth fairly literally.[25] As Mark Noll puts it, "Borrowing liberally from Old Testament precedents, many early Americans and not a few in more recent days have regarded the United States as God's New Israel, a nation established in this New World Canaan as a land flowing with wealth and freedom."[26]

A persistent element has been the notion of Americans as God's chosen people. Thomas Jefferson originally proposed that the national seal of the United States should represent the people of Israel led into the promised land by the pillar of light.[27] For the country's first major historian, George Bancroft, the United States was God's chosen nation, a foil of Europe, feudalism, and Old World atavism.[28] For novelist Herman Melville, "We Americans are the peculiar chosen people—the Israel of our time."[29] Abraham

Lincoln referred to Americans as the Almighty's "almost chosen people."[30] For their part, southerners before the Civil War saw themselves as God's New Israel, and even after their defeat saw redemption for their lost cause if they kept the faith.[31]

Historical writing about the United States has taken note of its religious underpinnings. Walter Russell Mead writes, "For Americans, there was little doubt from the beginning that they were chosen by God. The Puritans believed themselves to be the elect of the elect. English Protestantism was the fullest flowering of God's true religion."[32] Daniel Howe, author of an authoritative history of the United States between 1815 and 1848, observes, "Like the ancient Israelites, the Americans had wrested their homeland from other occupiers, believing that this action fulfilled a divine purpose."[33] For the Mexican historian, Edmundo O'Gorman, "In the north...there was an ever-increasing feeling that the new lands did not mean a providential gift from God to the motherland, but rather a providential opportunity to exercize religious, political, and economic liberty, so hindered and fettered in the Old World. So...every group saw in its own portion of the new lands and in its own peculiar way of life the New Jerusalem come true."[34]

Religion continues to play an important role in American life. American presidential inaugural addresses are replete with the invocation of civil religion. The evangelical movement, with its literal, even apocalyptical interpretation of the Bible, accounts for some 30 to 40 per cent of the American population.[35] Its influence on the American political right has been enormous in recent decades. Some, such as Kevin Phillips, have interpreted this as a move to an American theocracy. Others see it as the consecration of the ongoing religious underpinnings of American life as compared to contemporary Western Europe, where secularism, at least among the non-immigrant population, is the dominant motif.[36] Either way, *Habits of the Heart,* to cite an important study of American religious beliefs,[37] continue to be an essential part of the American story, and providentialism is a persistent element in the American dream.

In the case of New France, some of the same missionary zeal deployed by the Spanish (and Portuguese) in Latin America was directed toward the indigenous peoples. The Jesuit Missions are a vital part of the history of the French settlement, with figures such as Father Brébeuf martyred by the Iroquois a testament to the power of the faith. In the post-Conquest period, the Church became a dominant institution, coming in its more intransigent, ultramontane forms to mould the educational and social institutions of French-Canadian society between 1840 and 1960. Claims of a special divine mission were not lacking: "When you have reflected upon the history of the Canadian people, it is impossible not to recognize the great designs of Providence that presided over its formation.... The mission of the American France upon this continent... [is to be] the sole apostle of the true faith in North America... to lead back under the aegis of Catholicism the errant peoples of the New World."[38]

The Church was successful in restricting freedom of speech, the press, education, and even conscience during its long period of ascendancy in French Canada.[39] Comparisons with Mexico come to mind, especially the domination of the Church in New Spain and its key part in defining Mexican identity into the early twentieth century. The Church in Quebec lost a good deal of its sway only in the aftermath of the Quiet Revolution of the 1960s. Anti-clericalism grew in the 1960s, when Pierre Vallières, an intellectual associated with the radical Front de Libération du Québec (FLQ), described the Church as the witch of God.[40] With this transformation came the move to greater secularism and pluralism in the self-definition of Quebec society. It is no accident, perhaps, that Quebec's (and Canada's) leading philosopher, Charles Taylor, himself a believer, has entitled a recent major book *A Secular Age*.[41]

In English-speaking Canada, the notion of a chosen people found expression from time to time in the vision of Canada's unique destiny as an offshoot of the British Empire. For Bishop Strachan, the leading Anglican cleric of Upper Canada (Ontario) in the 1820s and 1830s, the British were God's second chosen people, with Canadians as their offspring.[42] Egerton Ryerson, writing about the War of 1812, argued that "The Gideon hordes of loyal Canadians repelled and scattered, for more than two years, the Midian and Amalekite thousands of democratic invaders."[43] The Fathers of Confederation in the 1860s, casting about for a name to describe the new Canadian federation, hit upon the term dominion, derived from the Book of Psalms (72.8). If not quite a new Jerusalem, Canada would be the manifestation of the dominion from sea onto sea that God would give to its inhabitants. "The Methodist church sought to make Canada the natural home for the kingdom of God on earth. It therefore sought to Christianize and civilize all its subjects, including new immigrants and the native population, and thereby make the nation a proper dominion for the Lord."[44] Subsequently, Canadian Methodists in their missionary activities both in Canada and abroad saw themselves (much as their American counterparts did) as carrying out God's work here on earth.[45] For his part, George Munro Grant, Principal of Queen's University, wrote in 1897, the year of

Victoria's Diamond Jubilee, "We have a mission on earth as truly as ancient Israel had. . . . Our mission was to make this world the home of freedom, of justice, and of peace, and to secure these ends the British Empire was the highest secular instrument the world had ever known."[46] So the historian W.L. Morton may well have been right in highlighting the importance that religion, more than wealth or politics, played in the lives of both French and English Canadians in the Victorian era when he said that "God and the Church were very present actors in the World."[47]

English Canada has seen a weaker role for organized religion in public life since World War II. The fact that Canada has a significantly smaller evangelical movement than the United States helps explain why policies on abortion or same sex marriage have been reflective of a more secular set of values at the national level. In British Columbia the percentage of the population professing "no religion" has approached 35 per cent in recent censuses, a North American high. One major caveat, however: there has been a strong evangelical presence in the Conservative Party, the governing party of Canada since 2006, and with it has come pressure for the instillation of more traditional family values in Canadian society accompanied by greater public religiosity than before.[48]

Thus, religion played an important part in the forging of New World national identities. The Mexican Grito de Dolores (Cry of Independence) of 1810 proclaimed, "Long live Our Lady of Guadalupe! Death to bad government! Death to the *gachupines* [peninsular Spaniards]!" One thinks of phrases like "In God we Trust" or "So help me God" in the United States, or the language of the Battle Hymn of the Republic, replete with its biblical imagery. The French version of O Canada, invokes both the cross and the faith.[49] A crucifix presides over the proceedings in Quebec's National Assembly to this day. And there is reference to God in the Preamble to the Canadian Charter of Rights dating from as recently as 1982.

Is it a coincidence that the notion of chosen peoples turns out to be a feature common to all three North American countries? It built on their European origins and religious roots, providing a vehicle for distinguishing Creoles and European settlers from indigenous peoples, as well as providing a form of legitimacy for the conquest and settlement that followed. Throughout history, conquest has been the key instrument of imperial development and state building. Those who conquer frequently make claim to some higher civilizing mission—far more noble than the crude pursuit of wealth and power. And religion—as evident in the biblical story of the Israelites and Canaan, the rise of Islam from the seventh century on, the

Crusades of the Middle Ages, and the competing credos of the Reformation and the Counter-Reformation—can provide the necessary ballast. We may live in a more secular age—at least in the West—but that was hardly true of previous centuries, and we fool ourselves to underestimate religion's deep emotional appeal, not least to those who crossed the great ocean separating New World from Old. As William James, the American pragmatist and philosopher of religion, noted in his journal, "Religion in its most abstract expression may be defined as the affirmation that all is not vanity."[50] Religion was a vital element in the European settlement of the continent and a key wellspring for national identities in the three states that came to make it up.

Notes

1 Cited in Brent Gilchrist, *Cultus Americus: Varieties of the Liberal Tradition in American Political Culture, 1600–1865* (Lanham: Lexington, 2006), 236.

2 Charles Sanford, *The Quest for Paradise: Europe and the American Moral Imagination* (Urbana: University of Illinois Press, 1961), 40.

3 Lafaye, *Quetzalcoatl and Guadalupe*, 304.

4 Lafaye, *Quetzalcoatl and Guadalupe*, 258.

5 D.A. Brading, *Mexican Phoenix: Our Lady of Guadalupe* (Cambridge: Cambridge University Press, 2001), 146.

6 Brading, *Mexican Phoenix*, 257.

7 José G. Merquior, "The Other West: On the Historical Position of Latin America," *International Sociology* 6, no. 2 (June 1991): 149–64, 154.

8 Robert N. Bellah and Steven M. Tipton, eds., *The Robert Bellah Reader* (Durham: Duke University Press, 2006), 516.

9 Ross, *El Monstruo*, 59.

10 Samuel Ramos, *Profile of Man and Culture in Mexico* (Austin: University of Texas Press, 1962), 79.

11 Frank Tannenbaum, *Peace by Revolution: Mexico after 1910* (New York: Columbia University Press, 1933), 47.

12 Daniel Cosío Villegas, *American Extremes* (Austin: University of Texas Press, 1964), 37.

13 Cited in Will Fowler and Peter Lambert, eds., *Political Violence and the Construction of National Identity in Latin America* (New York: Palgrave Macmillan, 2006), 40.

14 Cited in Michael C. Meyer and William L. Sherman, *The Course of Mexican History*, 5th ed. (Oxford: Oxford University Press, 1995), 543.

15 David C. Bailey, *¡Viva Cristo Rey! The Cristero Rebellion and the Church-State Conflict in Mexico* (Austin: University of Texas Press, 1974).

16 Hugh O'Shaughnessy, "Pope acts against incest priest's group," *Independent*, August 8, 2010, http://www.independent.co.uk/news/world/americas/pope-acts-against-incest-priests-group-2046517.html, accessed December 18, 2011.

17 Roberto Blancarte, "Religion, Church, and State," in *Changing Structure of Mexico*, ed. Laura Randall (Armonk, NY: Sharpe, 2006), 431.

18 Louis Baritz, *City on a Hill* (New York: John Wiley, 1964), 17.

19 Cited in Sacvan Bercovitch, *The American Jeremiad* (Madison: University of Wisconsin Press, 1978), 60.

20 In Conrad Cherry, ed., *God's New Israel: Religious Interpretations of American Destiny* (Chapel Hill: University of North Carolina Press, 1998), 57.

21 Perry Miller, *Errand into the Wilderness* (Cambridge, MA: Harvard University Press, 1956), 147.

22 Nathan Hatch, "The Democratization of Christianity and the Character of American Politics," in *Religion and American Politics*, 2nd ed., ed. Mark Noll and Luke Harlow (New York: Oxford University Press, 2007), 93–94.

23 "God has promised us a renowned existence, if we will but deserve it. He speaks this promise in the sublimity of Nature.... It is uttered in the thunder of Niagara. It is heard in the roar of two oceans.... His finger has written it in the broad expanse of our inland seas." James Brook, "The Knickerbocker," 1835, cited in Miller, *Errand into the Wilderness*, 210.

24 Sacvan Bercovitch, "The American Jeremiad," in *American Social and Political Thought: A Concise Introduction*, ed. Andreas Hess (Edinburgh: Edinburgh University Press, 2000), 86.

25 Richard Niebuhr, cited in Sanford, *The Quest for Paradise*, 88.

26 Mark A. Noll, *A History of Christianity in the United States and Canada* (Grand Rapids: William Eerdmans Publishing, 1992), 405–06.

27 Berndt Engler and Oliver Scheiding, eds., *A Companion to American Cultural History: From the Colonial Period to the End of the 19th Century* (Trier: WVT Wissenschaftlicher Verlag Trier, 2009), 254.

28 Joyce Appleby, *Liberalism and Republicanism in the Historical Imagination* (Cambridge, MA: Harvard University Press, 1992), 12.

29 Herman Melville, *White Jacket* (New York, 1850), chap. 36.

30 Abraham Lincoln, Address to New Jersey State Senate, February 21, 1861, http://teachingamericanhistory.org/library/index.asp?document-1062, accessed December 18, 2011.

31 Kevin Phillips, *American Theocracy* (New York: Viking, 2006), 143.

32 Walter Russell Mead, *God and Gold: Britain, America and the Making of the Modern World* (New York: Knopf, 2007), 311.

33 Daniel Walker Howe, *What Hath God Wrought: The Transformation of America 1815–1848* (New York: Oxford University Press, 2007), 855.

34 Edmundo O'Gorman, *The Invention of America: An Inquiry into the Historical Nature of the New World and the Meaning of its History* (Bloomington: Indiana University Press, 1961), 144–45.

35 Paul Moyer, cited in Phillips, *American Theocracy*, 253.

36 John Micklethwait and Adrian Wooldridge, *God is Back: How the Global Revival of Faith is Changing the World* (New York: Penguin, 2009).

37 Robert Bellah et al., *Habits of the Heart: Individualism and Commitment in American Life* (New York: Harper and Row, 1986).

38 Abbé Casgrain, cited in André Siegfried, *The Race Question in Canada* (Toronto: Carleton Library, 1966), 175.

39 Siegfried, 42.

40 Pierre Vallières, *White Niggers of America* (Toronto: McClelland and Stewart, 1971), 176.

41 Charles Taylor, *A Secular Age* (Cambridge, MA: Harvard University Press, 2007).

42 S.F. Wise, "God's Peculiar Peoples," in *The Shield of Achilles*, ed. W.L. Morton (Toronto: McClelland and Stewart, 1968), 53.

43 Noll, *A History of Christianity*, 407.

44 Neil Semple, *The Lord's Dominion: The History of Canadian Methodism* (Montreal: McGill-Queen's University Press, 1996), 442.

45 "[Methodists] profoundly believed that Christianity was the only true religion and that God demanded its adoption throughout the world," Semple, *The Lord's Dominion*, 442; see also Ruth Compton Brouwer, "Canadian Protestant Overseas Missions," in *Empires of Religion*, ed. Hilary Carey (London: Palgrave, 2008).

46 Cited in Carl Berger, *The Sense of Power* (Toronto: University of Toronto Press, 1970), 219.

47 Cited in Noll, *A History of Christianity*, 546.

48 Marci McDonald, *The Armageddon Factor: The Rise of Christian Nationalism in Canada* (Toronto: Random House, 2010).

49 "Car ton bras sait porter l'épée, Il sait porter la croix...Et ta valeur, de foi trempée, Protégera nos foyers et nos droits." (Because your arm knows to wield the sword, it knows to bear the cross...and your valour, steeped in faith, will protect our homes and our rights.)

50. Cited in John Jacob Kaag, "Pragmatism and the Lessons of Experience," *Daedalus* 138, no. 2 (Spring 2009): 63–72, 66.

THREE

Trajectories to Independence

"Deep is the well of the past."
—*Thomas Mann*[1]

The path a people follows to achieve its independence can have lasting implications. Struggle against an outside power can engender a sense of empowerment; internal divisions can haunt a polity; an ambiguous sense of identity can undermine a common sense of purpose. Succeeding generations may find themselves following unconsciously in the footsteps of those who came before.

It was in the eighteenth century that the Spanish and British colonists began to see their identities as essentially "American,"[2] but the forms this would take differed significantly among them. In the North American context, there can be no gainsaying the path-breaking character of the American Revolution. Here was the first instance of a New World society fully breaking its connection with the old one. Here was a revolutionary discourse that talked the language of rights, liberty, constitutionalism, individualism, and republicanism.

The American Revolution was above all a political and not a social one. It built fulsomely on the experience of the colonial assemblies, a well-established legal system, religious pluralism, and the high level of literacy. (Hundreds of thousands of copies of Thomas Paine's 1776 pamphlet *Common Sense* were sold to a population of 3 million!) It did not challenge institutions of property or put into question the commercial, no less than agricultural, underpinnings of the 13 Colonies.[3] Still, it was, in the words of the historian George Wood, "the most radical and far-reaching event in American history."[4] And the itinerary that the 13 Colonies followed, from independence to the establishment of the American Constitution, had dramatic implications for the larger Atlantic world and for the North American continent in particular.

To be sure, the stain of slavery tarnished the American experiment through the first seven decades of the country's existence and left an ongoing legacy of racism that has not vanished to this day (despite the election of Barack Obama, the first African-American president, in 2008). The differences between North and South over slavery and its potential extension westwards culminated in a momentous civil war, memorialized in the phrase in Lincoln's Second Inaugural address about "every drop of blood drawn with the lash...paid by another drawn with the sword."[5]

Nonetheless, the experience of 1776–83 and the establishment of a republican system of government through the Constitutional Convention of 1787 reinforced currents in monarchical France—an ally of the colonists in their struggle against the British—pushing for the transformation of that Old World state, a process that culminated in the French Revolution. It acted as a beacon for the Creoles of Spanish America, helping to precipitate a cascade of independence struggles in the first decades of the nineteenth century. And it was a signal to the British in their administration of their empire to press ahead with timely reforms such as responsible government in their remaining British North American colonies by mid-nineteenth century.

The revolutionary path the Americans had chosen laid the groundwork for American exceptionalism. The United States declared its independence from Britain not only politically but in a deeper civilizational sense. The American Constitution, with its federal structure and separation of powers, was the first modern republican constitution. The 1801 election was the first example of a peaceful transfer of power between political parties in a liberal democratic state. Economically, though dependent on British capital for some of its early ventures, the United States blazed a trail of its own, commercially, industrially, and technologically. In religion, Americans did not follow only the old doctrines, proving remarkably amenable to sects and denominations of all kinds, such as the Seventh Day Adventists and the Mormons, and to a constitutionally entrenched separation of church and state. Demographically, the United States was a haven for millions who poured in from Europe (and subsequently Asia and Latin America), coming to constitute not only the first "new nation," as Seymour Martin Lipset called it,[6] but the first melting-pot nation.

American exceptionalism has not always been a force for the good. Southern exceptionalism and racism have constituted an ongoing legacy since the days of slavery. Successive waves of immigrants, from Irish and Italians to Chinese, East Europeans, and Latinos, have experienced the barbs of American nativism. The American labour movement has had a hard time overcoming fierce opposition from the captains of industry and their political allies—something that may help explain both the absence of a socialist or social democratic party in the United States (unlike other English-speaking countries, not to speak of continental European ones) and the lamentably weak position in which organized American labour finds itself today.[7] In terms of social policy, the United States has been a laggard when compared to most other Western countries. And in its foreign policy, a sense of its superior mission has too often gone hand in hand with a pursuit of imperial interests of its own, e.g., during the Mexican-American War, the Spanish-American War, and the Cold War era in Latin America and Southeast Asia.

On the positive side, the United States has been spared the polarizing political extremes of continental European or Asian states, e.g., full-blown fascism or Marxism-Leninism. Slavery aside, it avoided the divisions of status and class derived from a feudal order and with it the social stigmatization that long haunted Old World societies. Its economic dynamism has made the country the trailblazer in the development of an affluent society, with labour-saving devices and mass consumption goods widely available. It has been a pioneer in popular education and mass culture, and its leading institutions of higher learning and research are among the finest in the world.

American political institutions—separation of powers, federalism, presidentialism, judicial review, constitutional paramountcy, popular sovereignty—have served as paradigmatic ones for many countries elsewhere. They are legacies of the American trajectory to independence, of the United States following a path of its own choosing, turning its back proudly, nay defiantly, on Old World models. And the two other North American societies have been strongly influenced—both positively and negatively—by its course.

During the roughly three centuries of Spanish domination, Mexico was ruled by 62 viceroys "almost all [of whom] came from the high nobility and were born in Spain."[8] Mexico had not been prepared for independence, given the absence of colonial assemblies of the type found in the 13 Colonies, and this resulted in what Alexander von Humboldt termed "a defect of sociability," what in contemporary parlance we might call a weak or non-existent civil society. The Counter-Reformation that dominated New

Spain may well have contributed to a cultural vitality as evidenced in religious architecture, or, more arguably, to a better integration of indigenous peoples than in the United States,[9] but it did little to lay the basis for the Enlightenment-derived debates that influenced American intellectual discourse or for the political leap forward that independence entailed.

The 11-year struggle for Mexican independence ended in 1821. Even then, deep divisions persisted between conservatives and liberals, with much political instability and frequent military coups the norm. Internal divisions help explain Mexico's vulnerability vis-à-vis the United States, leading to its defeat in the Mexican-American War of 1846–48 and the loss of about half of its former territory. Although the Constitution of 1857 had a decidedly liberal tone to it, Mexico (like other Latin American countries) suffered from empty constitutionalism. Constitutions meant little in a country in which the French briefly foisted the Austrian Maximilian onto a make-belief throne as Emperor between 1862 and 1867, and where, shortly thereafter, Porfirio Díaz came to monopolize power until 1911.

The shaping of Mexican identity took a more dramatic, chaotic, and violent form with the Mexican Revolution. A grandiose affair, stretching out over the period 1910–17, the Revolution has been subject to varying interpretations. Some have insisted on its ultimately middle-class character, with the liquidation of an older Mexico in favour of a modern state.[10] Others have celebrated the Constitution of 1917 as the first modern constitution to consecrate social rights side by side with individual ones.[11] Still others have invoked the egalitarian and communitarian passion that characterized the Revolution, symbolized by peasant demands for the return of their lands.[12] This comes closer to the genealogical meaning of revolution—*revolvere*, that is, returning to something that had previously existed or regaining long-lost rights—of which one also finds traces in the English Revolution of the mid-seventeenth century (overthrowing the Norman yoke) or in the French Revolution (restoring the liberty of the ancient Franks). Still others have contrasted the bold promises of the Constitution of 1917 with the more sober reality of institutionalized power and administrative corruption that was to follow.[13] Nonetheless, both the Revolution and the Constitution of 1917 are hallmarks of Mexico's modern *raison d'être*.

Progressive features included the distribution of land through *ejidos,* holdings collectively owned by the peasantry; the nationalization of petroleum by President Cárdenas in 1938; the need of Mexican governments to accommodate some of the social demands coming from the working class (especially from the CTM, *Confederación de Trabajadores de México,*

Confederation of Mexican Workers), peasantry, and middle class; cultural creativity in the 1920s and 1930s most notably; and the modernization of Mexico through the twentieth century under state aegis, though with the growing role of big business, both Mexican and foreign, especially American.

The negatives of post-revolutionary Mexican history are not to be overlooked. These include deep religious divisions in the 1920s culminating in the *Cristeros* revolt of 1926–29; endemic violence and lawlessness in different regions of the country of which narco-trafficking is but a current manifestation; the role of *caciques,* or regional bosses, and associated oligarchies in keeping Mexican states under their thumb; a top-down structure of power, concentrating an inordinate amount of power in the office of the presidency; and one-party domination (by the Party of the Institutionalized Revolution or PRI) until 2000 and the debatable honesty of several of the seriously contested presidential elections, e.g., in 1929, 1988, and 2006.

One might be tempted to argue that earlier features of Mexican history persist, despite globalization, the coming of NAFTA, or the ending of the PRI monopoly over power in 2000. The uneven process that led to the country's initial break with Spain, Mexico's often conflicted relationship with the United States, and varying strands within its own Revolution—from progressive to authoritarian—have left a shadow over much that has come since. More than many other modern nation-states, Mexico continues to struggle with the spectre of its past.

Canada pursued a non-revolutionary road to independence. Its political leaders and population believed in British rather than American forms of liberty, dispensing with revolutionary breaks and mixing representative government and due process with the symbolism of monarchical institutions. Confederation was much less a parting of the ways with Britain than a form of Home Rule in Canadian domestic matters, with an ongoing series of ties to the mother country and its empire. Loyalism was an important part of the English-Canadian mentality until after World War II, and traces of it still linger in the retention of the British monarch as the Canadian head of state to this day. On the French-Canadian side, the question of survival as a national community was ever-present from the British Conquest on, imparting at times a melancholic note to national discourse.[14] By and large, French-Canadian national identity took a conservative, even counter-revolutionary form, with clerical influence prevalent until the early 1960s. (Here parallels with Mexico, both in the era of Spanish rule and in the century that followed its independence, are quite striking.) French-English divisions have been an ongoing feature of Canadian history, surfacing at the time of the Riel (or Métis) Resistance of the 1870s and 1880s, over the Manitoba and Ontario School Questions, during the conscription crises of both world wars, and with the emergence of a strong nationalist and subsequently separatist movement in Quebec after 1960. Internal dualism has lead to a recurring need to reconcile differences, e.g., conscription if necessary, but not necessarily conscription during World War II; the establishment of a Canada Pension Plan and a distinct Quebec Pension Plan in the 1960s; the Cullen-Couture Accord giving the Quebec government significant leeway over immigration in the 1970s; and the 2006 House of Commons resolution recognizing the Québécois as constituting a nation within a united Canada. Tensions can never be permanently resolved to the satisfaction of either side, but they need to be managed—for better or for worse.

Like its southern neighbour, Canada has been a country of immigration (and significant emigration to the United States). This has transformed its nature, both with the opening of the West and with the gradual decline of British ascendancy within the Canadian population as a whole. Economically, Canada remained within the shadow of the United States, especially as the twentieth century unfolded. Culturally, strong American influence has continued to make itself felt, despite earlier British and French influences and significant Canadian contributions. To this can be added fairly close political and military alignment with the United States during the two world wars, during the Cold War, and within NATO (the North Atlantic Treaty Organization) and NORAD (North American Aerospace Defence Command).

Canada has had a slow, evolutionary development as a country—political developments in the years 1791, 1840, 1848, 1867, 1931, 1949, 1965, 1982 come to mind. Its political traditions have been non-revolutionary, nay counter-revolutionary, unlike the American or Mexican experiences. As a result, gradualism and moderation have been the hallmarks of Canadian identity, both at home and abroad; e.g., peacekeeping and multilateralism have been the key elements of Canadian foreign policy for much of the postwar period. Still, gradualism and moderation domestically make for a rather tepid version of national identity, something that marks Canada to this day.

In the modern period, civic identity has increasingly won out over ethnic in both English-speaking Canada and Quebec. But whose version of civic will come to prevail? Canada's? Quebec's? The Charter of Rights and Freedoms has been important as a unifying element for English-speaking

Canada, most tellingly as a source of civic identity in the post-colonial era in spite of all the ambiguity and opposition patriation and the battle over the Charter elicited in many quarters in Quebec. No less important for the francophone majority in Quebec, however, has been Bill 101, the Charter of the French Language, passed by a resolutely nationalist Quebec government in 1977. Old fault lines do not disappear with the coming of the Internet or the liquid modernity[15] of our age. Canada's is inevitably a less robust version of national identity than that of its southern neighbour.

All three North American countries share European colonial pasts, followed by the eventual eclipse of the European empires that presided over their early destinies. As New World societies, all have had reasons to look to their constitutions in cementing their national identities. There the similarities end. Americans are heirs to a quite original political system, forged after their Revolution, which, for all its imperfections, has survived with only minor changes for well over two centuries. English Canadians have not been given to bold leaps as a people, being adepts of British liberty with its mixed constitution and finely modulated, ordered nuances. Overall, they have tended to be more deferential to authority than their American counterparts, only recently acquiring a written Charter of Rights. For their part, French Canadians, in Alexis de Tocqueville's words, were a defeated people,[16] defensive by instinct, and therefore late-comers in their embrace of pluralism and modernity. They have always been marked by a sense of national identity distinct from their English-speaking counterparts. Mexicans bear the historical marks of a hierarchically defined society, of a divided polity in its quest for independence, of a country lacking political stability for a good part of the nineteenth century, only to be followed by a more authoritarian presidential style of politics until very recently. However, they have the legacy of a revolution that marked their passage into modernity and of a constitution that has at least held out the promise of greater social justice.

The paths the three countries pursued in becoming sovereign states continue to shape their national identities centuries later. And the distinctiveness of these paths ensures that there is little by way of a common North American consciousness, or of what the French historian Pierre Nora has called *lieux de mémoires* (realms of memory) to bind North Americans together.[17] Instead, we have *lieux de mémoires* that are exclusively Canadian (the Plains of Abraham, the War Memorial in Ottawa, the Last Spike at Craigellachie, Vimy Ridge); exclusively American (Bunker Hill, the Statue of Liberty, Gettysburg, Monticello, the Alamo, the Golden Spike in Utah);

or exclusively Mexican (the Pyramids of the Sun and Moon at Teotihuacan, the shrine of Our Lady of Guadalupe, Mexico City's Zócalo, Oaxaca's Mount Albán, Yucatan's Mayan ruins). Here may lie the real Achilles heel to any would-be framing of a larger North American ensemble.

Notes

1 Thomas Mann, *Joseph and his Brothers*, trans. H.T. Lowe-Porter (New York: Knopf, 1948), 3

2 Elliott, *Do the Americas Have a Common History?*, 38.

3 "[F]ewer scholars would contend that the American Revolution of the eighteenth century was itself a social upheaval of the European type." Louis Hartz, "The Nature of Revolution," *Society* 42, no. 4 (2005 [1968]): 54–61, 57.

4 Gordon Wood, cited in Godfrey Hodgson, *The Myth of American Exceptionalism* (New Haven: Yale University Press, 2009), 30.

5 Abraham Lincoln, *Second Inaugural Address*, http://www.bartleby.com/124/pres32.html, accessed December 16, 2011.

6 Seymour Martin Lipset, *The First New Nation: The United States in Historical and Comparative Perspective* (New York: W.W. Norton, 1979).

7 Robin Archer, *Why is There no Labor Party in the United States?* (Princeton: Princeton University Press, 2007).

8 Meyer and Sherman, *The Course of Mexican History*, 155.

9 Merquior, "The Other West," 153.

10 Meyer and Sherman, *The Course of Mexican History*, 269, 309.

11 "The Constitution of 1917 is the legal triumph of the Mexican Revolution, the first great social upheaval of the twentieth century." E.V. Niemeyer Jr., *Revolution at Querétaro: The Mexican Constitutional Convention of 1916–1917* (Austin: University of Texas Press, 1974), 233.

12 "The Mexican Revolution was popular and instinctive. It was not guided by a theory of equality; it was possessed by an egalitarian and communitarian passion. The origins of this passion lie, not in modern ideas, but in the traditions of indigenous communities before the Conquest and in evangelical Christian missions.... Peasants demanded the return of their lands." Octavio Paz, *Itinerary: An Intellectual Journey* (New York: Harcourt, 1994), 22.

13 "One of the sources of pride of my generation lay in the fact that the Mexican Constitution had been the first in the world to consecrate social rights side by side with individual ones. Articles 27, 123, 130 were exemplary.... Later, I learned that constitutional articles do not apply forever, and do not mean the same thing all the time.... The same constitution which sustained Calleo [in the late 1920s and early 1930s] served Cardénas in establishing a government

more representative of the Mexican revolution." Enrique Pedrero, *La cuerda tenso: apuntes sobra la democracia en México, 1990–2005* (Mexico, DF: Fondo de Cultura Económica, 2006), 231. "The achievements of the Mexican Revolution in pursuing its three major objectives: political liberty, agrarian reform, and labor organization have been neither slight nor meagre ... a general administrative corruption has spoiled the whole program of the Revolution." Villegas, *American Extremes*, 18.

14 Jocelyn Maclure, *Quebec: The Challenge of Pluralism* (Montreal: McGill-Queen's University Press, 2003), chap. 1.

15 The sociologist Zygmunt Bauman "argues that liquid modernity is experienced as speeding, fleeting and transitory and liquid modern men and women are in effect disembedded from what sociologists might have once upon a time called the local community." Tony Blackshaw, *Zygmunt Bauman* (Milton Park: Routledge [Key Sociologists], 2005), 102.

16 Alexis de Tocqueville, *Regards sur le Bas-Canada* (Montreal: TYPO, 2003).

17 Pierre Nora, *Realms of Memory: Rethinking the French Past* (New York: Columbia University Press, 1996).

FOUR

"Language Has Always Been the Perfect Instrument of Empire"

"Now is the time and this is the country in which we may expect success in attempting changes favorable to language, science and government."
—Noah Webster[1]

In 1492, Antonio de Nebrija, a Spanish humanist, published the first grammar of the Spanish language, dedicating the book to Isabella the Catholic, Queen of Spain. When he presented it to her, she asked, "Why would I want a work like this, I already know the language." To this de Nebrija answered, "Majesty, language is the perfect instrument of the empire."[2]

Language can be central to a people's identity. A large majority of European states are associated with a specific language, and the very name of their inhabitants coincides with that of the language they speak—e.g., Dutch, English, French, German, Italian, Spanish, Polish, Russian, Swedish. In East Asia, as well, the connection between national identity and language can be very close—China, Korea, and Japan come to mind. What about the New World and the North American continent in particular?

The languages native to the New World were those of its indigenous peoples. Some were spoken by members of relatively small tribes, others such as Nahuatl or Mayan became the mode of communication of large-scale civilizations. As languages of empire, they not only overwhelmed those of subject peoples, they developed forms of pictorial writing of a highly sophisticated character, such as the Aztec codices.

These, however, are not the languages that prevail in North America today. Instead, the languages of one-time European empires—Spanish, British, and French—have come to dominate. They have done so, however, in a peculiar way. Far removed from European metropolitan centres and courts, settlers in the New World found themselves forced to account for phenomena equally removed from Old World habitats.

Flora and fauna were significantly different. Tomatoes, corn, cocoa, and tobacco were New World plants; armadillos, buffaloes, caribou, coyotes, skunks, turkeys, and quetzals were creatures native to North America. Rivers, lakes, mountains, canyons, deserts, plains—all needed names, a fair number of them borrowed from the continent's indigenous peoples. Words such as canoe, hammock, moccasin, powwow, and totem are indigenous in origin.

The prevailing pattern was one first of imposition, then of adaptation of the language of empire to the new colonies. In the case of Nueva España, as Mexico would be known before its independence in 1821, the Church played an important role in the widespread dissemination of Spanish. *Hablar en cristiano*—to speak as a Christian—became a synonym for linguistic and not merely religious conversion of the indigenous population.[3] The elites of colonial Mexican society, both Spanish-born and Mexican-born (Creole), looked to Spain for their linguistic models.[4] At the same time, "the Mexican Spanish language of the Mestizo majority, besides having incorporated hundreds of Indian (mainly Nahuatl) words, often had intonations which denoted the native languages' influence."[5]

As the formal political ties between Mexico and Spain were severed, Mexican Spanish increasingly acquired a vocabulary and diction of its own. Octavio Paz noted in his *Labyrinth of Solitude* that "For us, writing means breaking down the Spanish language and re-creating it in such a way that it becomes Mexican without ceasing to be Spanish."[6] Betraying something deeper about the Mexican mentality is the extensive vocabulary describing death. The philologist Lope Blanch lists some 2,500 entries for the word, and Claudio Lomnitz sees it as a metonymic sign of Mexicanness itself.[7]

On a less mordant note, one need but refer to a contemporary dictionary of "Mexicanisms," with its thousands of entries, to see how far the Mexicanization of Spanish extends. Political examples include the term *antireeleccionismo,* referring to opposition to the re-election of existing officials, of particular significance because of the long tenure of Porfirio Díaz, Mexican president and dictator between 1876 and 1911; *dedazo* describing the designation of his successor by the incumbent president (figuratively pointing his finger at him), during the twentieth-century one-party reign of the PRI; *ir al otro lado,* literally going to the other side, referring to going or migrating to the United States; and *malinchismo,* from the name of Cortes's indigenous concubine Malinche, referring to those with a complex for embracing foreign models and downplaying indigenous ones. Other examples are *mariposa monarca,* the monarch butterfly that migrates in the millions between Canada and Mexico every year, and *chipotle,* a variety of chili that requires no more translation than *taco* or *Tabasco.*[8]

What was true for Spanish in Mexico proved equally so for English in the United States. The speech of succeeding generations of settlers might be marked by the different regions of Britain from which they had come,[9] but increasingly American speech deviated from that of Britain, and American English took on a life of its own.

Symbolically, the break came in 1828, some 50 years after the American Revolution, with the publication of Noah Webster's *American Dictionary of the English Language.* The mere fact that the dictionary was now being called American rather than English underlined the divergent paths American and British English had begun to follow. As Webster stated in his Preface, "A great number of words in our language require to be defined into a terminology accommodated to the condition and institutions of the people in these states.... It has been my aim in this work...to provide a standard of our vernacular tongue which we shall not be ashamed to bequeath to three hundred millions of people who are destined to occupy...the vast territory within our jurisdiction."[10] It is striking to see that Webster could envisage an American population of 300 million back in 1828. It is also quite clear that his dictionary project, with its simplification of spelling and emphasis on American speech, reflected a deeper nationalist agenda. As he also noted in his *Preface,* "Language is the expression of ideas, and if the people of one country cannot preserve an identity of ideas, they cannot retain an identity of language.... In no two countries of the earth remote from each other, can such an identity be found."[11]

The Publication of Webster's dictionary heralded only the beginning. Writers such as Emerson, Melville, Hawthorne, Whitman, and Twain did much to develop an American literature in the nineteenth century, shaping the English language to their own needs. The opening stanza of Whitman's *Song of Myself* epitomizes this nativist quest. "My tongue, every atom of my blood, [is] formed from this soil, this air."[12] With progressive waves of immigrants, American English was also influenced by words borrowed from German, French, Spanish, Italian, Swedish, Dutch, Yiddish, and many others.[13] American and British terminology grew further and further apart. A few illustrations from H.N. Mencken's 1927 *The American Language* are listed below.[14]

American	British
apartment	flat
corn	maize
editorial	leader
French fries	chips
janitor	porter
pantry	larder
race track	race course
sweater	pull-over

Place names, while often originally derived from British home places or figures—New England, New York, New Jersey, Virginia—came to be increasingly varied as settlement moved westwards. Influences from other languages were common, from French in the Mississippi Valley and Louisiana, Dutch in New York, German in Pennsylvania, and Spanish in the Southwest (as well as biblical names such as Beulah, Canaan, Sharon, and Jordan).[15] Vernacular American expressions were another important innovation with colloquialisms such as "to cave in," "fork over," and "barking up the wrong tree," as well as ungrammatical expressions such as "used to could" and "there's no two ways about it." Well could Rudyard Kipling, like other Old World visitors to the United States, sneeringly note in 1890, "Their speech is becoming a horror already.... The American has no language. He is dialect, slang, provincialism, accent, and so forth."[16] But it was the speakers of American English, not British English, who ultimately prevailed, and American intonation and pronunciation became the templates for global English.

The explanation for this is directly linked to the rise of the United States to world power status. Asked in 1899, the year of his death, which single factor would most shape the twentieth century, Otto von Bismarck replied, "The fact that the Americans spoke English." A shrewd observation from the German Iron Chancellor, for let us just imagine what the nature of alliances in World War I might have been had Americans spoken German or what the language of globalization today might be. The influence of American culture—cinema, music, art, literature—both high-brow and popular—increased dramatically at the international level as the twentieth century proved to be, in Henry Luce's prophetic words, an American century.[17] This was helped along by the decline of the old European empires, including the British, and cemented by the dominant military, economic, political, and technological role the United States came to play in world affairs after 1945. With this new global ascendancy came a decline of other languages, relatively speaking. German lost its ascendancy in Central and Eastern Europe in the aftermath of the defeat of the Third Reich. French found itself increasingly on the defensive, even within the institutions of the European Union, once this was expanded to include its current 27 members. Russian enjoyed a short-term advantage due to Soviet domination over Eastern Europe, a situation that melted away after 1989. To the degree that language has historically been an instrument of empire, as Antonio de Nebrija had informed Queen Isabella in 1492, the empire over which the Americans presided had American English as its primary mode of communication. Or perhaps, we should call this *globish,* the language of globalization and of the modern age, spoken by some 1.5 billion people around the world. In the words of Max Lerner, "There is scarcely a non-English-speaking country...in which the desire to learn English has not become an urgent one: it is as if the legend of American wealth and influence has made it a kind of *lingua franca* over a large part of the globe."[18]

Canada's has been a binational experience of empire. New France creatively borrowed from Indian languages for place names (such as Canada and Quebec) and for flora and fauna ("*orignal* for moose, *caribou* for a genus of large deer"[19]). The reduced sense of hierarchy from what prevailed in France led to greater informality, e.g., the use of *tu* over *vous.* Place names reflected the fauna and flora of the New World, e.g., Pointe aux Alouettes, Cap à l'Anguille, Rivière du Caribou, Rivière au Rat Musqué.[20] After the British Conquest, an English-speaking commercial elite came to dominate, with telling implications for the French language. Alexis de Tocqueville, visiting in 1831–32, noted that in both Montreal and Quebec City, "all the signs are in English and there are only two English theatres." During his visit to the courthouse in Quebec City, Tocqueville observed the predominance of the English language and the mediocrity of the language of French-speaking lawyers, which was riddled with Anglicisms. On the basis of these observations he concluded bluntly, "it is easy to see that the French Canadians are a conquered people.... I have never been more convinced than after I left the courthouse that the greatest and most irreversible tragedy for a people is to be conquered."[21]

French Canadians were able to overcome the assimilationist intentions toward their language articulated by Lord Durham in his Report after the failed 1837 rebellions and to achieve political domination within Quebec at the time of Canadian Confederation. Still, English retained its high status within the province for the next century and greatly influenced the development of Quebec French, especially its more colloquial form known as *joual*.

Resentment over the dominant position of both English and Anglophones within Quebec society played an important part in fuelling the nationalism of the Quiet Revolution. A powerful expression of this is contained in Michèle Lalonde's poem of the 1960s "Speak White," recalling the *hablar en cristiano* attitude that had prevailed in colonial Mexico.[22]

The upshot of the political ferment of the period was a series of provincial bills dealing with language, in particular Bill 101, the Charter of the French Language, establishing French as the official language of Quebec and ensuring its predominance in the province's educational system, workplace, and public sphere. Yet the seductive power of English in Quebec has not been reduced, nor would it be even if Quebec were to become a sovereign state tomorrow. The overweening presence of the United States next door, economic ties with Canada, and the importance that English has assumed at the global level (e.g., through the Internet) will continue to influence Quebec society. At best, language policies such as Bill 101 provide territorial security for French within Quebec's borders, even as its inhabitants have been forced to accept the reality of American English as the imperial language all around them.[23] After all, as the authors of *The Story of French* have noted, "Historically, French Canadians and Acadians have been dealing with the imposing local presence of English for centuries."[24]

One further observation. The evolution of Quebec French has paralleled those of English, Spanish, and Portuguese in the New World in its growing differentiation from the version of the language spoken in Europe.[25] The result is a whole series of terms and words specific to Quebec. The *Dictionary of Canadian French* contains 240 pages of such words and terms. And it also underlines grammatical differences between Quebec and European French, with regards to the use of gender, pronouns, verbs, and negation.[26]

Quebec	France
Les États	les États-unis
Arrêt	Stop
déjeuner	petit déjeuner
arachide	cacahouète
huard	plongeon imbrin
scab	jaune, briseur de grève

What about English-speaking Canada? Canadian English was histori-cally something of a hybrid of British and American, with regards to spell-ing for instance. With Canada located in North America and with many of its original English-language settlers, the Loyalists, as well as many of the subsequent settlers of western provinces having migrated from the northern United States, the die was cast where the evolving pronuncia-tion of Canadian English was concerned. For all the British influence on political institutions and economic links through finance capital, it was the proximity of Jefferson's empire of liberty that dictated the future of Canadian English. The Fathers of Confederation may have opted for Brit-ish over American liberties during the Confederation Debates, and it wasn't until the 1920s that American capital displaced British as the primary source of foreign capital in the country, but Canada was something of a canary in the mine where the displacement of British by American English was concerned. From the nineteenth century on the majority of Canadians have been speaking a North American form of English, not a British Eng-lish. Canada moved effortlessly from the British to the American sphere nowhere more seamlessly than in the realm of language, as shown for instance in the choice of popular magazines. Here, language preceded eco-nomic and political developments. As Robert McCrum describes it in *The Story of English*, "Canadian English is another regional variant of American English."[27] For Raven McDavid Jr., who updated Mencken's classic study of American English, "American mass communication and supermarket culture are among the major forces shaping Canadian speech for better or for worse."[28]

This is not to deny the existence of distinctly Canadian terms in the English language. Examples include Anglophone, francophone, sov-ereignist, First Nation, Status Indian, postal code, RCMP, RRSP, term deposit, heritage language, social insurance number (SIN), snow route, Lotus Land, butter tart, smoked meat, and Nanaimo bar.[29] There is also a Quebec English vocabulary, with its use of French words such as *autoroute, colloque,* or *dépanneur* that have little currency outside Quebec.[30] Still, Ste-phen High hit the nail on the head when he argued that "One is struck not so much by the differences between American and Canadian English today as by the similarities.... One can conclude only that these small differences were exaggerated to serve as markers of national distinctiveness at a time of intense national anxiety and nation building."[31] When Canadians find themselves abroad, there can be little doubt to themselves or others that the English they speak is North American in character.

Further evidence of the linguistic sway of the United States within North America is associated with the evolving fate of Spanish. Ever since the late nineteenth century, as the Mexican ethnologist Manuel Gamio observed, the Spanish spoken in the northern border region of Mexico has been strongly influenced by English.[32] This has become far more the case since World War II, as "Spanglish" is spoken along the Mexican-American border and tens of millions of Mexicans and Latinos have moved to the United States. Code switching between English and Spanish, hybrid language forms, and the wholesale importation of American terms into Mexican Spanish have become the norm.[33] Examples include *parquear* for "to park," *chequear* (to check), *surfear* (to surf), and *quitear* (to quit); advertisements in Mexico contain phrases such as "Tips para marketing."[34] Latinos living in the United States are far more prone to the linguistic influence of English. According to R.J. Stout, "Reflexive verbs... give way to cause and effect in imitation of English grammar.... In similar form, possession often hardens into the American form of identity."[35]

None of this poses any danger to Spanish as the dominant language of Mexico, but Spanglish (or "espangles") has its own way of insinuating itself into Mexican Spanish through popular culture, music, film, and the like. And since Mexico is the single largest Spanish-speaking country in the world, with significant publishing and media outlets that reach beyond its borders, it has become something of a transmission belt for Spanglish to the larger Spanish-speaking world.

There are two key conclusions to draw from this discussion. First, North American languages are the result of Old World contact with New World societies and of adaptation to them. As Octavio Paz observed,

> The European languages were rooted out from their native soil and their own tradition, and then planted in an unknown and unnamed world: they took root in the new lands and, as they grew within the societies of America, they were transformed. They are the same plant yet also a different plant. Our literatures did not passively accept the changing fortunes of the transplanted languages: they participated in the process and even accelerated it. They very soon ceased to be mere transatlantic reflections: at times they have been the negation of the literatures of Europe; more often, they have been a reply.[36]

What has been true for literature is even more true for popular or demotic speech. There was a greater informality to spoken Spanish, English, or French in the New World, which was as far removed as the settlers were from the courts and capital cities of the metropolises. *Tú* and *ustedes* rather than *tú* and *vosotros* became the familiar second person pronouns in Mexican Spanish; *tu* rather than *vosotros* became the familiar singular pronoun in Mexican Spanish;[37] and *tu* has displaced *vous* in colloquial Québécois French. The simplicity of speech that de Tocqueville observed in the mid-1830s United States spoke to a greater equality among inhabitants in the New World than in the Old. The story of European languages in North America may have begun as one of imposition through conquest and settlement, but adaptation to local circumstances, the absorption of words from indigenous languages, the influence of immigrants from a wide variety of backgrounds, and the need to invent new terms to describe evolving societies had the same result—a creolization of European languages, be they American or Canadian English, Mexican Spanish, or Québécois French.

Second, the political and military role of the United States as a superpower, combined with its cultural and economic dynamism, explain the rise of English to the status of a global language. Its dominant position within North America, given American demographic supremacy, has reinforced the leading position of English on the continent. The fact that it is also the dominant language spoken in Canada, with only minor differences from the American version, has further helped this along. And the penetration of English into French in Quebec through *joual* and the increasing penetration by Spanglish of Mexican border regions and beyond as commerce, migration, and mass tourism have grown, underline the fulsome reach of American English. In this, one can see a vindication of Antonio de Nebrija's prophecy about language being the perfect instrument of empire. Only the empire in question is now the American one, not the old European ones whose time has passed.

Notes

1 Noah Webster, "Dissertations," cited in *Simplified Spelling Society Newsletter* (Spring 1986): 20, 21. [Later designated *Journal 2.*]

2 Joshua A. Fishman, *European Vernacular Literacy: A Sociolinguistic and Historical Introduction* (Bristol: Multilingual Matters, 2010), 52.

3 Claudio Lomnitz, *Deep Mexico, Silent Mexico: An Anthropology of Nationalism* (Minneapolis: University of Minnesota Press, 2001), 21.

4 "In Mexico one finds words in perfect use long since moribund in Spain." *El Pais* (October 10, 2009): 72.

5 Miguel Leon-Portilla, *Mesoamerica 1492, and on the Eve of 1992*, University of Maryland Working Papers, Dept. of Spanish and Portuguese 1 (1988), 33.

6 Octavio Paz, *The Labyrinth of Solitude: Life and Thought in Mexico* (New York: Grove Press, 1961), 165.

7 Claudio Lomnitz, *Death and the Idea of Mexico* (New York: Zone Books, 2005), 26–27.

8 Guido Gómez de Silva, *Diccionario Breve de Mexicanismos*, lst ed. (Mexico: FCE, 2001).

9 Fischer, *Albion's Seed.*

10 Arthur Schalmon, ed., "Noah Webster's Preface to his Dictionary," in *Webster-isms: A Collection of Words and Definitions Set Forth by the Founding Father of American English* (New York: Free Press, 2008), 40, 42.

11 Schalmon, "Noah Webster's Preface," 39.

12 Walt Whitman, *Song of Myself*, section 1, in Walt Whitman, *Complete Poetry and Collected Prose* (New York: The Library of America, 1982), 188.

13 There are numerous examples given in H.L. Mencken, *The American Language*, 4th ed., with new material by Raven I. McDavid Jr. (New York: Knopf, 1963), 189–97, 251–66.

14 Mencken, *The American Language*, 267–317.

15 William Fowler, "American Dialects," in *The English Language* (1850), cited in Mencken, 104–05.

16 Rudyard Kipling, "At the Golden Gate," in *American Notes*, 1891, http://www.gutenberg.org/files/977/977-h/977-h.htm, accessed December 20, 2011.

17 Henry Luce, "The American Century," *Life Magazine*, February 17, 1941.

18 Max Lerner, *American as a Civilization* (New York: Simon and Schuster, 1957), 811.

19 Fischer, *Champlain's Dream*, 475.

20 André Lapierre, "Parcours toponymiques de l'Amérique française," in *Langue, espace, société*, ed. Claude Poirier (Ste. Foy: Presses de l'Université Laval, 1994), 227–35.

21 Cited by Claude Corbo, *Encyclopedia of French Canadian Cultural Heritage in North America*, www.ameriquefrancaise.org/en/article-466/Alexis_de_Tocqueville%E2%80%99s_visit_to_Lower_Canada_in_1831.html, accessed May 20, 2011.

22 Michèle Lalonde, *Speak White*, trans. Albert Herring, Albert Herring Everything Website, http://everything2.com/user/Albert+Herring/writeups/Speak+White, accessed May 20, 2011.

23 Cf. Jean Laponce, *Languages and their Territories* (Toronto: University of Toronto Press, 1987).

24 Jean-Benoit Nadeau and Julie Barlow, *The Story of French* (Toronto: Knopf, 2006), 234.

25 "Il y a un français québécois, comme il y a un anglais états-unien, un portugais brésilien. Ne pas le reconnaître, c'est nier toute notre histoire et la plus grande partie de notre culture de Nord-Américains." Noël Audet, *Entre la Boussole et l'Étoile* (Montreal: XYZ, 2006), 147.

26 Sinclair Robinson and Donald Smith, *Dictionary of Canadian French* (Toronto: Stoddart, 1990).

27 Robert McCrum et al., *The Story of English* (London: Faber and Faber, 1992), 263.

28 Mencken, *The American Language*, 469.

29 Laurel J. Brinton and Margery Fee, "Canadian English," in *The Cambridge History of the English Language*, Vol. VI, *English in North America*, ed. John Algeo (Cambridge: Cambridge University Press, 2001), 422–40, 434–38.

30 Brinton and Fee, "Canadian English," 438–39.

31 Steven High "The Narcissism of Small Differences—Canadian English" in Magda Fahrni and Robert Rutherdale, *Creating Postwar Canada* (Vancouver: University of British Columbia Press, 2008), 104.

32 Manuel Gamio, Mexican ethnologist, wrote in the 1920s that "The Spanish of Yucatan is a Maya-Spanish; that of the high plateaus influenced by Aztec or Otomi; that of Sonora by the speech of the Yaquis, that of Oaxaca by that of the Zapotecas; that of the North bordering the frontier by English." Cited in Patricia Funes, *Salvar la nacion* (Buenos Aires: Prometeo Libros, 2006), 279.

33 Rainer Goetz, *La lengua Española: Panorama Sociohistórico* (Jefferson, NC: McFarland, 2007), 198.

34 Gerald Erichsen, "Spanglish: English's Assault on Spanish," http://spanish. about.com/cs/historyofspanish/a/spanglish.htm, accessed May 20, 2011.

35 Robert Joe Stout, *The Blood of the Serpent: Mexican Lives* (New York: Algora, 2003), chap. 5.

36 Paz, Nobel Prize Lecture.

37 John M. Lipski, *Latin American Spanish* (London: Longman, 1994), 283.

FIVE

Manifest Destiny and the Fate of a Continent

"The whole continent of North America was destined by Divine Providence
to be peopled by one nation... in one federal union."
—*John Quincy Adams*[1]

One way of exploring the geopolitics of North America is through a straightforward version of action and reaction. The United States led the way in establishing sovereign territorial states in the Western Hemisphere. Successive expansion and consolidation made it a continent-sized country, and economic dynamism and population expansion established it as the dominant North American power, a position reinforced by its emergence in the twentieth century as a world power.

Accompanying the rise of the United States to its current position was the potent doctrine, messianic in character, of manifest destiny. It found early expression in the decades following the American Revolution. Jedediah Morse, a Massachusetts pastor, wrote in 1789, "It is well known that empire has been travelling from east to west."[2] Jefferson voiced expansionist thoughts in an 1801 letter to James Monroe when he wrote that "However our present interests may restrain us within our own limits, it is impossible not to look forward to distant times when our rapid multiplication will expand itself beyond those limits, and cover the whole northern, if not the southern continent, with a people speaking the same language, governed in similar forms, and by similar laws."[3] And he gave expression to the messianic impulse when he described the United States as "the solitary republic of the world, the only monument of human rights...the sole depository of the sacred fire of freedom and self-government."[4]

By mid-nineteenth century, with westward expansion underway and the Mexican-American War on the horizon, John Sullivan articulated what would become a key component of the American credo, evoking "our manifest destiny to overspread the continent allotted by Providence for the free development of our yearly multiplying millions."[5] Others were not slow to pick up the theme. For Brooks Adams, author of *The New Empire*, "The [United States] will outweigh any single empire, if not all empires combined. Commerce will flow to her from both east and west."[6] For Senator Albert Beveridge of Indiana, an important political figure at the turn of the twentieth century, "God has not been preparing the English-speaking and Teutonic peoples for a thousand years for nothing but vain and idle self-contemplation and self-admiration. No! He has made us the master organizers of the world to establish system where chaos reigns.... He has made us adepts in government that we may administer government among savage and senile peoples.... And of all our race he has marked the American people as His chosen nation to finally lead in the regeneration of the world."[7] The American historian, Charles Beard, was right to sense a darker force behind this expansionist ideology when he wrote that "It is an illusion to think of Americans as a pacific people; they are and always have been one of the most violent peoples in history."[8]

Both Canada and Mexico have had to come to terms with the reality of American expansionism and manifest destiny. The inhabitants of British North America had little choice but to look to Britain for their protection. They were fortunate that Britain was the leading world power in the nineteenth century, able to defeat the United States in the War of 1812 and maintain control over the westernmost portion of British North America in the Oregon Boundary Dispute of 1846–48.[9] The American Civil War and the accompanying Fenian raids into Canada hastened the move to Confederation, with the British Empire providing a limited security umbrella for the newly formed Dominion of Canada. By the end of the nineteenth century, Britain and the United States had grown sufficiently close that direct conflict between them over Canada would have been an anomaly. (The Alaska Boundary settlement of 1903 was to prove this; it gave the Americans control over the entire Alaska Panhandle, with the British arbitration board member, Lord Alverstone, siding with the Americans, who had threatened to get their way by force if necessary.[10])

A number of factors helped Canada preserve its position as an independent North American state. One, quite simply, was the fact that Canada's northern location, much of it tundra and rocky terrain unsuitable for agricultural settlement, did not make it an attractive venue for the inhabitants of the American Atlantic seaboard states in their westward expansion. Another factor was linguistic and cultural propinquity. French Canadians aside, the inhabitants of nineteenth-century British North America/ Canada were predominantly English-speaking Protestants. Loyalists fled New England, New York, and Pennsylvania for Ontario, Quebec, and the Maritimes, but their values and those of their descendants, when it came to public education, homesteading, or commercial activity, were not all that different from those of their American neighbours. They too were wedded to a system of common law, notions of private property, elected legislatures and responsible government, and a federal distribution of powers. They preferred a monarchical to a republican form of government, putting greater emphasis on peace, order, and good government (British liberties) than on individual liberty and constitutional rights (American liberties), but they also subscribed to a continental version of a dominion from sea to sea, with a railway to tie the regions together, close in spirit to what the Americans had devised. They were no less racist and exclusionary toward Oriental immigration than their American counterparts and no less caught up with delusions about the superiority of the Anglo-Saxon peoples in the heyday of such ideas at the end of the nineteenth and beginning of the twentieth centuries.[11] And, like Americans, they were given to a pragmatic outlook, more interested in what could work in the here and now than in pursuing grandiose schemes or ideals.

Still, Canadians were not prone to invoke the language of manifest destiny in thinking of their own future. Some, such as George Munro Grant or George Robert Parkin, embraced the idea of an imperial federation, with Canada as a sort of junior partner to Britain within the empire, helping to shape its overall policy. But this was never more than a pipedream. Few in Britain would ever have accepted such a transformation; Quebec would have adamantly rejected such a vision of Canada's external role; and the empire, in any case, soon began to decline. The United States proved the rising power in the twentieth century. If French Canadians were long concerned about *la survivance* within a federal system where they constituted a permanent minority, Canadians as a whole—constituting less than 10 per cent of the American population—had to find their own way of surviving the potential blandishments of American power within the continent. As late as 1911, Champ Clark, the Speaker of the American House of Representatives, stated, "I hope to see the day when the American flag will float over every square foot of the British North American possessions...."[12]

Fear of American annexation only began to weaken in the twentieth century. The Loyalist past dissipated and in its place came the celebration of the long undefended border. Canada's military alliance with the United States during the latter half of the two world wars, followed by NATO and NORAD in the postwar period, further consecrated the new ties. In more recent times, some have appealed to the concept of an *Anglosphere,* fuzzy ties supposedly binding together English-speaking peoples, in the same way that Spanish speakers have at times invoked *Hispanidad* or French-speakers *la Francophonie.*

Still, the sheer size and weight of the American presence on the continent have posed a continuing challenge to Canadian identity, a sense of having to navigate the shoals of proximity with caution. Harold Innis in 1951 wrote about the need to resist American imperialism in all its attractive guises.[13] The novelist Hugh Maclennan captured the ongoing mixture of ambiguity and tenacity that has characterized Canadian attitudes to the United States:

> [F]or nearly a hundred years the nation had been spread out on the top half of the continent over the powerhouse of the United States and still was there.... Canadians of United Empire Loyalist origin have never been easy in their conscience that their ancestors made the right choice in 1776.... In the back of their minds and in the back of many Canadian minds which think in English lurks the notion that we can 'join the States.' But this we cannot do for a multitude of reasons and in their heart all realistic Canadians know it.[14]

Prime Minister Lester Pearson paid the price for daring to publicly criticize American policy in Vietnam, receiving a dressing down from President Lyndon Johnson for his pains. Prime Minister Pierre Trudeau evoked the mouse and the elephant analogy,[15] suggesting that Canada's margin of autonomy from the United States was in the 15 to 20 per cent range. The Canada-United States Free Trade Agreement and NAFTA pointed towards greater continental integration, and they were followed by the closing-in of the American border after 9/11 with, for example, passports required for Canadians entering the United States. Canada stayed out of an American-led military venture in Iraq, though its involvement in Afghanistan was a gauge of goodwill in the years that followed. So there is a constant to and fro in Canada's relationship with the United States, one that dominates Canadian foreign policy to an overwhelming degree.

Mexico proved less successful in resisting American manifest destiny, since a large chunk of future American territory was originally part of New Spain. Texan independence between 1836 and 1845 heralded the process, with the Mexican-American War of 1846–48 resulting in the present-day Southwest and California coming into American possession. The American marines acquired a marching song, "From the Halls of Montezuma," based on the short-term American occupation of Mexico City in 1847. More conscience-driven Americans acknowledged the flimsy basis for this feat of arms, Ulysses Grant declaring it "one of the most unjust wars ever waged by a stronger nation against a weaker nation,"[16] and John Quincy Adams stating, "In this war, the flag of honor and justice will belong to Mexico, and the American flag, I am ashamed to say, will stand for dishonor and slavery."[17] The war engrained in the Mexican collective consciousness a sense of hopelessness about their country's fate, what the nineteenth-century Mexican liberal journalist, Guillermo Prieto, described as living in a "homeland of tears."[18] Living side by side with a dangerous neighbour made Mexico "the booty of the United States...the first (modern nation-state) to shudder at the spectacle of an untimely death."[19] Hence the resentment of American commercial and political domination that bubbled up at the time of the Mexican Revolution and its aftermath. Hence also a tendency for Mexican intellectuals for a long period of time to be more oriented towards Europe or Latin America than North America in their search for an authentic Mexican path through the labyrinth of identity. According to philosopher Leopolda, "Latin America is the daughter of European culture; it is the product of one of its major crises.... From Europe we have received our cultural framework, what could be called our structure: language, religion, customs, in a word, our conception of life and world is European. To become disengaged from it would be to become disengaged from the heart of our personality."[20]

Mexico came more clearly into its own after 1910. Nationalism dominated in the 1920s and 1930s, as the increasing Mexicanization of the economy and takeover of powerful American interests led to a period of strained relations with the United States. Relations improved during World War II and the decidedly pro-American turn under the administration of Miguel Alemán (1946–52) and most of his successors. Cross-border migration and remittances back home from Mexicans working in the United States were an important reason for this. Mexican elites increasingly went to the United

States for their higher education and leisure activities. NAFTA was the culmination of this *acercamiento* (rapprochement). Still, Mexico, not unlike Canada, cultivated its independence from the United States by retaining good relations with Cuba after its Revolution, opposing the 2003 Iraq War, and maintaining ties with Latin America and with the Organization of Ibero-American States. Whatever attractions North American integration may hold for Mexicans are balanced by a desire for autonomy *vis-à-vis* the American hegemon.[21]

Survival—*la survivance*—has been a leitmotif of both English and French Canada and of Mexico in different ways. Since emerging from under the shadow of the British Empire, Canada has cultivated its cultural autonomy, through institutions such as the CBC (Canadian Broadcasting Corporation), the National Film Board, and the Canada Council for the Arts. Quebec went through its own cultural effervescence in the decades following the Quiet Revolution, which began in 1960. Expo '67 marked the centennial of Confederation, and in the decades that followed the proclamation of the Charter of Rights and Freedoms and patriation of the Constitution helped give the country a clearer sense of identity as an officially bilingual and multicultural country in the northern part of the continent. On the other hand, there have been repeated internal crises over the threat of Quebec separation, and although Canada has achieved high rankings in United Nations Human Development Reports, and remains somewhat more Atlanticist/European in its political culture than its neighbour to its south, the reality of living cheek by jowl with the United States constitutes an ongoing challenge.

Mexico survived the American territorial grab of mid-nineteenth century and a short-lived French encroachment during the Archduke Maximilian episode of the 1860s. The Revolution of the 1910s set the country on an independent course. Still, as Daniel Cosío Villegas noted in a widely cited postwar essay,

> If we judge the present situation of Mexico with any degree of severity, it is difficult to avoid the conclusion that the country is passing through a most serious crisis...if it is underestimated or ignored...it will end by Mexico entrusting its major problems to inspiration, or to imitation of and submission to the United States.... We would call on that country for money, for technical training, for patterns in culture and art, for political advice; and we would end up by adopting unchanged its whole scale of values, so alien to our history, our interests, and our tastes.[22]

And as Alan Riding has observed, "Nationalism and even anti-Americanism are natural by-products of the relationship, serving Mexico both as an aggressive response to the past and as a defensive shield against the present. It is not an ideological reaction. Successive governments, whether left-wing or conservative, have felt duty-bound to articulate a nationalist posture, not only to camouflage deeply felt frustration and impotence at Mexico's dependence, but as a way of strengthening a sense of national identity."[23]

Before one can contemplate any kind of deeper North American integration, along the lines of the European Union for example, one first has to come to terms with the unequal power relations among the three countries. Unlike Europe, where no single power bestrides the continent, North America is a continent dominated by the United States. That leaves the citizens of North America's two other nation-states (or state-nations) in the uncomfortable position of placing a far greater premium on their bilateral relationship with their dominant neighbour than on any other aspect of their foreign policy. As Carlos Fuentes has noted, "In the world in which we live, Mexico will always have problems with the United States."[24] To which many Canadians would say "Amen."

There are benefits, to be sure, flowing from the cordial relations between Canada and the United States for over a century and from the reasonably good ones between Mexico and the United States at least since mid-twentieth century. More than is true of any of the other major continents, North America has been the home of democratic peace. But under the surface lie old memories of American expansionism, territorial appropriation, and fears of too close an entanglement. The fact that both Canada and Mexico have survived the periodic threat of absorption by the United States is itself something of a miracle. And North America, despite American manifest destiny, remains a continent made up of three countries—not one.

Notes

1 Cited in Robert Kagan, *Dangerous Nation* (New York: Knopf, 2006), 130.

2 Cited in Engler and Scheiding, *Companion to American Cultural History,* 253.

3 Engler and Scheiding, *Companion to American Cultural History,* 263.

4 Robert W. Tucker and David C. Hendrickson, *Empire of Liberty: The Statecraft of Thomas Jefferson* (New York: Oxford University Press, 1990), 7.

5 John L. Sullivan, *Democratic Review* (1845); cited in Deborah Madsen, *American Exceptionalism* (Edinburgh: Edinburgh University Press, 1998), 89.

6 Brooks Adams, *The New Empire* (New York: Macmillan, 1902), 18.

7 Cited in Rogers Smith, *Stories of Peoplehood* (Cambridge: Cambridge University Press, 2003), 117.

8 Cited in Giovanni Arrighi, *Adam Smith in Beijing* (London: Verso, 2007), 247.

9 Howe, *What God Hath Wrought*, chap. 18: "Westward the Star of Empire."

10 Thomas A. Bailey, "Theodore Roosevelt and the Alaska Boundary Settlement," *Canadian Historical Review* 28, no. 2 (June 1937): 123–30.

11 Edward Kohn, *This Kindred People: Canadian-American Relations and the Anglo-Saxon Idea, 1895–1903* (Montreal: McGill-Queen's University Press, 2004).

12 Mapleleafweb, 1911 Federal Election in Canada, http://www.mapleleafweb.com/voter-almanac/1911-federal-election-canada, accessed May 15, 2011.

13 Harold Innis, "The Strategy of Culture," quoted in Donald Creighton, *Harold Adams Innis, Portrait of a Scholar* (Toronto: University of Toronto Press, 1957), 143.

14 Hugh Maclennan, *Two Solitudes* (Toronto: McClelland and Stewart, New Canadian Library), 470; also Hugh Maclennan, "After 300 Years, Our Neurosis is Relevant," in *Canada: A Guide to the Peaceable Kingdom*, ed. William Kilbourn (Toronto: Macmillan, 1970), 11.

15 "Living next to you, is like [a mouse] sleeping with an elephant; no matter how friendly and even-tempered is the beast, one is affected by every twitch and grunt." Prime Minister Pierre Trudeau, speaking to the Washington Press Gallery in 1969. Cited by Lydia Miljan in her review of Bruce Muirhead, *Dancing around the Elephant: Creating a Prosperous Canada in an Era of American Dominance, 1957-1973*, in *Canadian Journal of Political Science* 41, no. 1 (March 2008): 237.

16 Ulysses S. Grant, cited in Bruce Cumings, *Dominion from Sea to Sea: Pacific Ascendancy and American Power* (New Haven: Yale University Press, 2009), 68.

17 John Quincy Adams, cited in Ignacio Solares, *Yankee Invasion* (Minneapolis: Scarletta Press, 2009), 93.

18 Solares, *Yankee Invasion*, 75.

19 Lomnitz, *Death and the Idea of Mexico*, 28.

20 Leopoldo Zea, "The Actual Function of Philosophy in Latin America," in *Latin American Philosophy for the Twenty-First Century*, ed. Jorge Gracia and Elizabeth Millan-Zaibert (Amherst: Prometheus, 2004), 361, 363.

21 Cf. Josefina Zoraida Vázquez and Lorenzo Mayer, *México frente a Estados Unidos: 1776–2000* (Mexico: FCE, 2001).

22 Vallegas, "Mexico's Crisis," in his *American Extremes*, 23.

23 Riding, *Mexico*, 329.

24 Carlos Fuentes in Karim Bitab and Robert Fadel, eds., *Regards sur la France* (Paris: Seuil, 2007), 212.

SIX

Market Society and Possessive Individualism

"A net full of holes is our legacy to you
passengers of the twenty-first century. The ship is sinking for lack of air,
there are no more forests, the desert
shimmers in an ocean of greed."
—*José Emilio Pacheco*, City of Memory[1]

In many ways, North America, even more than Europe, has been the continent of market capitalism. Commercial values were deeply implanted in the 13 Colonies, even before the creation of the United States. In Benjamin Franklin's words, "Get what you can, and what you get hold;/'Tis the Stone that will turn all your Lead into Gold."[2] Individualism and enterprise were among the cardinal values on which the United States was founded.[3] Alexander Hamilton, the first Secretary of the Treasury, embodied the pursuit of commercial values and protected manufacturing industries while his more agrarian-oriented opponent, Thomas Jefferson, came to accept the importance of commercial interests in a republic that celebrated the free individual.[4]

Public enterprise—or more correctly, publicly subsidized enterprise—has not been lacking in the United States, as Felix Rohatyn for one has noted in referring to the construction of the Erie Canal and the creation of the Land Grant colleges, the Tennessee Valley Authority, and the Interstate Highway System.[5] But from its inception the United States has been a country where businessmen, not politicians, have shaped the economy.[6] And the ideology of business, from the tycoons of the Gilded Age in the late nineteenth century to the CEOs of modern-day American corporations, has generally hued to the line articulated by Charlie Wilson, President of General Motors in the 1950s and then Secretary of Defense in the Eisenhower Administration: "What is good for the country is good for General Motors and vice versa."[7]

From this comes the well-known debate, dating from the early twentieth century, about the absence of socialism in the United States when compared with Europe.[8] And the fact that American populism, rooted in the Midwest, the West, and the South, was never able to break what the turn-of-the-twentieth-century Democratic politician William Jennings Bryan called "the cross of gold"[9] or impose more than limited regulatory reforms on the railways, grain companies, oil companies, and financial institutions of the country.

Despite Woodrow Wilson's New Freedom, Franklin Delano Roosevelt's New Deal, and Lyndon Johnson's Great Society, the privileged position of business in American society has scarcely been in jeopardy. Emerson's insight, dating from the mid-nineteenth century, captures a deeper reality: "Trade is the lord of the world nowadays—and government only a parachute to this balloon. There is nothing more important in the culture of man than to resist the dangers of commerce. Out of doors, all seems a market."[10]

The Canadian political philosopher C.B. Macpherson coined the term "possessive individualism" to define the values that come to characterize market societies as they developed from the seventeenth century on. Focusing on the works of Thomas Hobbes and John Locke, he argued that mainstream liberal theory has always had a strong property foundation to it, one that can lead to the justification of unlimited accumulation.[11] It would be wrong to claim that the United States has put no barriers in the way of such accumulation. After all, both personal and corporate income taxes attest to limits in this regard, despite the numerous loopholes built into the system.

Nonetheless, the pursuit of wealth seems to be built into the American psyche. At the time of the Revolution, Americans faulted the poor themselves rather than bad luck or God's will for their misfortune.[12] Henry Adams, the prominent New England writer, was lamenting the corruption of the republic by wealth by the late nineteenth century.[13] Friedrich Engels in 1887 wrote that America was "where no medieval ruins bar the way, where history begins with the elements of bourgeois society."[14]

As Michael Kimmage observes, "Enthusiasm for business and technology was an organic aspect of nineteenth-century American culture. The entire pattern of settlement in the American West, with the government perpetually lagging behind the settlers, made for an unusual relationship between the economy and the state and was woven into the myth of American individualism, upon which Goldwater and Reagan were both virtuosic improvisers."[15]

A study shows that almost 40 per cent of Americans today think that they are or can be in the top 1 per cent of income earners.[16] (This was before the Occupy Wall Street movement in fall 2011 helped publicize the divide between the 1 per cent who own much of the country's wealth and the 99 per cent who do not!) The reality is a level of inequality in the United States that exceeds that of most other Western countries.[17] There have been ups and downs over time, but in recent decades there has been a tendency for wealth to be concentrated in the top 1 per cent—and even more pointedly—in the top 0.1 per cent of the population.[18] As David Leonhardt has noted, "For most of the last three decades, tax rates for the wealthy have been falling, while their pre-tax pay has been rising rapidly. Real incomes at the 99.99th percentile have jumped more than 300 per cent since 1980. At the 99th percentile—about $300,000 today—real pay has roughly doubled."[19]

Under the circumstances, one needs to ask the question whether the United States is quite the middle-class society the majority of the population believes it to be. Horatio Alger legends aside, upward mobility in American society today is lower than in Europe.[20] It is also the case that the American social net is decidedly weaker than that of most other OECD countries.

James Bryce, author of *The American Commonwealth* and a British ambassador to the United States, stated that class divisions do not seem to be important there.[21] Author Joan Didion, who grew up in Sacramento, was told by her mother, when she was asked by her daughter to what class their family belonged, "Class is not a word we use."[22] Clinton Rossiter, a prominent political scientist of the postwar period stated, "Classes in America are stages rather than castes.... The best of all classes—in many ways the only class that counts—is the middle class."[23]

One of the characteristics of American exceptionalism, and a very potent one at that, has been the ability to make the logic of capitalism and markets seem natural in a way that has not been true in most other parts of the world. (I emphasize "seem" for, as Godfrey Hodgson has argued, the actual history of class conflict in the United States has not been all that different from that in Europe. Robin Archer has shown that repression has loomed larger in American labour history than in Australia's, helping to explain the absence of a Labor Party in the United States.[24]) Self-reliance, thrift, work, and wealth accumulation have been built so powerfully into the American body politic that they have become almost unchallengeable. Ideologically, the American labour movement, as Joyce Appleby notes, "started with a deficit, relying, as it must, on collective action in a nation that celebrates the individual, even though it was the giant corporations that did most of the employing."[25] To deride the rise of a leisure class, as Thorstein Veblen did at the turn of the twentieth century,[26] or lambaste the emergence of an American power elite, as C. Wright Mills did in the mid-twentieth century,[27] was to place yourself beyond the pale of respectability.

While American capitalism has been open to challenge on a whole range of specific points—from monopolistic practices to consumer protection to environmental degradation—it has been much less questioned as a dominant economic system. So deeply entrenched are its proponents, from every local and state service organization all the way to national associations that lobby on their behalf, that one is tempted to conclude that capitalism is as innate to the United States as the consumption of hamburgers, Coke, or apple pie. As a nineteenth-century English traveller noted, "He had never 'overheard Americans conversing without the word DOLLAR being pronounced.' It didn't matter whether the conversation took place 'in the street, on the road, or in the field, at the theatre, the coffee-house or at home.'"[28] As Larry Bartels observes, "Psychologists have spent considerable scholarly energy elaborating 'just world' or 'system justification theories.' Their basic idea is that 'living in an unpredictable, capriciously unjust world would be unbearable...so we cling defensively to the illusion that the world is a just place.' In the economic realm, one result is a widespread belief in the basic fairness of capitalism, even among people who seem to be at the losing end of the free-market system."[29]

What about Canada and Mexico? Given the influence of the dynamic neighbour they share, we might assume a similar pattern of capitalist values in both societies. Yet the story of each has been more complex and the result a more checkered view of the role that capitalism has come to play in North America.

Economic development in Canada was significantly more dependent on European powers than was that of the United States. In the case of New France, the court played a signal role in the exploration and settlement of the colony. A number of merchants in Normandy and western France provided capital of their own for the fur trade and related ventures. What was missing in New France, by and large, was the entrepreneurial element that was to prove so important in the 13 Colonies. As Daniel Johnson, Quebec Premier between 1966 and 1968, lamented during a visit to France, "If Richelieu and Louis XIV had allowed the French Protestants to settle in the New World...these émigrés would have easily dominated the English merchants of New England."[30] The result for Quebec, from the time of the British Conquest in 1759 to the Quiet Revolution of the 1960s, was a situation in which French Canadians played a secondary role in the major transportation, commercial, industrial, and resource developments of the province, with Anglophones and Anglophone enterprises holding the leading positions. The mentality of the traditional French-Canadian entrepreneur was far more family-oriented than expansionary, more provincial in focus than Canada-wide or beyond: "I don't want to get too big. I'm happy so long as I get a comfortable living for myself and my family.... It's no use being a millionaire in the cemetery" (shoe manufacturer); "I never made business with the bank. I have always used my own money. I pay cash" (furniture manufacturer).[31]

On the English-Canadian side, the exploitation of staples—cod, fur, square timber, wheat—for export to Europe was the prevailing feature of the Canadian political economy into the late nineteenth century. The exploitation of minerals, pulp and paper, and oil and gas—albeit with the United States as the primary export market—similarly characterized the Canadian political economy of the twentieth and early twenty-first centuries.

However, Canadians were not condemned to the proverbial role of hewers of wood and drawers of water evoked in the Old Testament (Joshua 9:23). Settlers from Britain and Loyalists from the 13 Colonies sparked the development of a Canadian-based capitalist elite, evidenced in companies such as the Northwest Company and the Bank of Montreal, which was founded in 1817. Canadian entrepreneurs were involved in fostering the development of canals and railways that were pivotal to the expansion of the Canadian economy across the continent. The building of the Canadian Pacific Railway and the hammering in of the Last Spike in 1886 became part of Canadian nation-building lore, celebrated in poetry, historical works, and TV drama.

A striking feature of Canadian development was its relatively concentrated character. For example, Canadian banks were far fewer in number and their charters more sparingly doled out by the federal government after 1867 than was true for their American counterparts. The Canadian tradition of safe banking, celebrated during the recent meltdown of American banking giants such as Lehman Brothers, can be traced back to this earlier oligopolistic tradition: "By the end of the first decade of the twentieth century,...Montreal and Toronto bankers [were] entrenched at the heart of finance capitalism in the country...a group of no more than 40 or 50 men presided over a financial community with assets of over $1.6 billion."[32]

Another feature was Canada's dependence on outside capital for its development. During the first 50 years after Confederation, much of this was British portfolio capital (i.e., bonds) that helped to fund infrastructural development. But American capital also began to spill over into Canada, prompted in part by the high tariff wall erected through the National Policy of 1878–79. By the 1920s, American capital had displaced British capital as the prime source of foreign investment, and the pattern did not change thereafter.[33]

Canadian capital was not confined to the financial sector or to a purely subordinate role. By the turn of the twentieth century, there were a number of important Canadian ventures abroad, e.g., the building and running of electric tramway systems in Mexico City and Rio de Janeiro, branches of the Bank of Nova Scotia in the Caribbean, and the export of farm implements by Massey-Harris. Canadian foreign investment abroad, while only a fraction of foreign investment in the country, prefigured the emergence of Canada by the second half of the twentieth century as a mature economy, one of the core countries of the capitalist world.

Were Canadian capitalists any less market-driven or profit-oriented than their American counterparts? Not really. But their entanglement with government, going back to the railway ventures of the late nineteenth and early twentieth centuries, has long persisted. At times, the state played a pivotal role in promoting economic development; consider the creation of Hydro Ontario as a Crown corporation in 1906, the nationalization of bankrupt lines to establish the Canadian National Railway after 1918, the founding of Trans-Canada Airlines in the 1930s, and the incorporation of Petro-Canada in the 1970s. There has been a symbiotic relationship between the corporate sector and government in this country.

The role of government has also been central to the creation of a larger French-Canadian controlled capitalist sector in Quebec since the 1960s. Hydro Quebec, much expanded as a state-run electricity grid after the nationalization of private companies in 1962, became a catalyst for French-Canadian economic activity. Significant financial resources were poured into the creation of enterprises controlled by French-Canadian entrepreneurs through the Caisse de Dépôt, the depository of contributions to the Quebec Pension Plan. The language legislation passed in 1977, Bill 101, helped to ensure a more salient role for French Canadians in the Quebec economy than before.

Is possessive individualism any less characteristic of Canada than of the United States? The Canadian economic landscape has had its share of mining tycoons and robber barons, large banks and corporate mastodons (the disgraced media mogul Conrad Black is but one modern example). Yet the degree of inequality in Canada today is somewhat less than that in the United States and the level of taxation and income redistribution is somewhat higher. As a study on income inequality in a range of countries notes, "The USA has the highest level of inequality of the Anglo Saxon countries, though Americans, if anything, lean towards favouring still more inequality relative to their Anglo-Saxon cousins. At the other end, the relatively low inequality Canadians lean, if anything, towards favouring still lower inequality relative to the rest of the group."[34] Another study of inequality in various Western societies also sees Canada as more egalitarian than the United States.[35] A note of caution, however. The share of the top 0.1 per cent of Canadian income earners increased from 1.2 per cent of the Canadian total in 1972 to 4.3 per cent in 2000. The share of the top 1 per cent of Canadian income earners increased from around 5 per cent in the late 1970s to over 10 per cent in 2000.[36] Inequality is clearly on the increase in Canada.

What about Mexico? The Spain that conquered the Aztec, Maya, and other peoples was a hierarchically organized, highly Catholic society, with feudal characteristics. The economic system constructed in the New World embodied most of these features. Tributary despotism and unequal exchange—not capitalism—characterized the relationship between Spanish and Creole on the one hand and Indians, blacks, and mulattos on the other.[37] "When the German explorer, Baron Alexander von Humboldt, showed up in the capital of New Spain in 1804, he counted 100 millionaires within the city limits, more than in any one city on the continent, but he was appalled by the sea of misery in which the masses were drowning. 'Mexico is the country of inequality,' he exclaimed."[38] As the Bishop of Morelia observed, "This country is divided between those who have everything and those who have nothing."[39]

Independence in 1821 did not mark the triumph of "bourgeois" over "feudal" features as much as "the removal of all vestiges of tributary despotism with its bureaucratic centralism, and the victory of large, semi-feudal landed property with its parochially oriented *caciquismo*."[40] When railways and resource-based ventures developed in Mexico toward the end of the nineteenth century, these were largely foreign-owned. For example, Americans owned 22 per cent of Mexico's land surface in 1910, including the most important mining, agriculture, and timber lands.[41] Worse yet, large numbers of indigenous people lived under de facto slavery into the early twentieth century, such as in the henequen plantations in the Yucatan Peninsula.[42]

The Mexican Revolution was partly about distributing land to landless peasants, but it also sparked the turn to a more important role for the state and to the eventual development of a more Mexican-based capitalist class. As Octavio Paz noted, "Without the Revolution and its leaders we would not even have any Mexican capitalists. National capitalism was not merely a natural consequence of the Revolution: to a great extent it was actually a creation of the revolutionary state."[43] This was particularly notable after 1940, when Mexico enjoyed an economic boom, the so-called Mexican miracle, albeit in the shadow of the United States. Monterey emerged as an agricultural economic powerhouse in the north, making family fortunes for some while others toiled in the fields. Provincial centres such as Guadalajara or Veracruz had their own economic elites, but Mexico City doubled as both the political and economic capital of the country.

In the postwar era Mexico began the transition to a more North American-style capitalist economy, at least where the middle and upper classes were concerned. American branch plants produced many of the most common consumer goods from soft drinks to toothpaste to breakfast cereals. The American economic model resonated through the appeals of advertising, film, and television. Mexico's GDP per capita and aggregate GDP showed a country achieving a Second World economy, if not quite a First World one.

Postwar Mexican elites were often American-trained. A number of presidents, including Miguel de la Madrid and Carlos Salinas, had Ivy League graduate degrees, and the same was true for their key economic advisors.[44] Alternative paths to power led through the Mexican branch plants of corporations such as Coca Cola—this was, for instance, Vincente Fox's perch as CEO of that company before his entry into politics in the 1980s and eventual accession to the presidency as the first successful opposition candidate in over 70 years.

The most striking feature of the Mexican economy when compared to those of Canada and the United States is the degree of inequality that prevails there: "Mexico's super-elite class includes at least 24 billionaires and 85,000 millionaires...both government statistics and UN Human Development Program statistics tell us that about 50 million Mexicans live in poverty on less than about $4 a day, while about 15 million live in 'extreme poverty,' on $1 or less a day."[45] In 1977 "the wealthiest 20 per cent controlled 54.4 per cent of the wealth, with the majority living in degrees of poverty ranging from mere survival to outright misery."[46] Nor had the numbers shifted much 30 years later, with the top 20 per cent accounting for 55 per cent of the wealth and the bottom 50 per cent accounting for only 18 per cent.[47] The level of literacy, despite significant government expenditures on public education, is low. Mexico figured 31 out of 32 in performance of its students in reading and math tests in an OECD study and 107 on a UNESCO list of its citizens' reading habits.[48]

It comes as no surprise therefore to learn that skepticism about the free market is significantly higher in Mexico than in the two other North American countries.[49] In 2005 fully 54.7 per cent of Mexico's population worked in the informal sector with no benefits or permanency of employment, as compared to only 8 per cent in a similar situation in Canada.[50] Millions of Mexicans in recent decades have been moving (or have attempted to move) to the United States in search of jobs and minimal incomes that elude them back home.

The Mexican conglomerate Televisa has become the largest media company in the Spanish-speaking world. Carlos Slim, whose telecom empire has made him the richest man in the world, has acquired a minority stake in *The New York Times*. But despite Mexico's 1994 accession to membership in the OECD—the club of First World economies—Mexico for many of its citizens remains a country divided between those who have everything and those who have nothing, with a smallish middle class in between. As George Grayson notes, "Self-serving policies permit Mexico's dominant class to live like princes, paying, at best, a widow's mite in taxes. They turn a blind eye toward improving education and health care—the primary factors for social development and economic mobility—while protecting the immensely wealthy and powerful moguls who fatten their foreign bank accounts thanks to the economic bottlenecks they have crafted, often with government collusion."[51] Writes David Lida, "Indeed, in Mexico City, where social divisions can be as pointillistic as in England, and a caste system is as firmly in place as in India, people with money perceive the poor as abstractions, blurs who only come into focus when they wait on them. The woman who comes to clean your home, the man who hands you a towel after you've washed your hands in the restroom, the guy in the yellow jumpsuit who sells you a phone card at the traffic intersection—you are certain these people exist because they've interacted with you."[52]

Another feature of Mexico's recent evolution is narco-trafficking. Drug gangs pose a serious threat to the stability of the country's political, economic, and social order, and lurid headlines of murders and decapitations in cities such as Ciudad Juárez or Nuevo Laredo have become the norm. The war on narco-trafficking declared by the Calderón government has brought no relief. This aspect of Mexico evokes the Mafia in Southern Italy far more than the norms prevailing in most First World states.

Overall, in thinking about the North American economy, it is clear that Canada and the United States have achieved a significantly higher level of capitalist development than Mexico. The possessive individualism one finds in the first two is an offshoot of market mechanisms and a market mentality, diluted to a degree by countervailing social and community norms. In the Mexican case, uneven distribution of wealth is grounded in a pre-capitalist system and mentality, which the Mexican Revolution and the postwar economic boom have not been able to entirely undo. Earnest protestations by successive presidents of their desire to alleviate glaring poverty have so far come to naught. More recently, Mexico has set off in pursuit of the same capitalist ideals that have characterized its two neighbours to the north, bringing it closer to the spirit of possessive individualism. And that may, with time, make Mexico more of a market society, a slightly more affluent society, though not necessarily any more just a society than Canada or the United States.

The challenge facing all three North American societies, as the current double-dip recession gripping much of the OECD suggests, is a serious rethinking of the way in which capitalist economies operate. High levels of unemployment, as in the 1930s, can wreak enormous political damage, while low rates of taxation of the wealthy or over-generous subsidies to banks and other powerful interests can generate their own resentments. The sustainability of economies dependent on cheap sources of energy—coal, oil, nuclear, each with its own drawback—is also very much in doubt. An ethic of unbridled capitalism is not only fundamentally unjust, it will not serve as an effective model for North America in a world economy careening out of control.

Notes

1 José Emilio Pacheco, *City of Memory and Other Poems*. Trans. David Lauer and Cynthia Steele. (San Francisco: City Lights, 1997), 33.

2 Peter Baida, *Poor Richard's Legacy: American Business Values from Benjamin Franklin to Donald Trump* (New York: W. Morrow, 1990), 25.

3 Peter H. Schuck and James Q. Wilson, "Looking Back," in Peter Schuck and James Wilson, eds., *Understanding America: The Anatomy of an Exceptional Nation* (New York: Public Affairs, 2008), 629, 631.

4 Joyce Appleby, *Capitalism and a New Social Order: The Republican Vision of the 1790s* (New York: New York University Press, 1984), 104–05.

5 Felix Rohatyn, *Bold Endeavours: How Our Government Built America, and Why It Must Rebuild Now* (New York: Simon and Schuster, 2009).

6 Alfred D. Chandler, "The Role of Business in the United States: A Historical Survey," *Daedelus* 98 (Winter 1969): 23–40.

7 Cited in Paul E. Peterson, "What is Good for General Motors," *Education Next* 9, no. 2 (Spring 2009), http://educationnext.org/what-is-good-for-general-motors/, accessed December 19, 2011.

8 Werner Sombart, *Why Is There No Socialism in America?* (London: Macmillan, 1976); Seymour Martin Lipset and Gary Marks, *It Didn't Happen Here: Why Socialism Failed in the United States* (New York: Norton, 2000).

9 "No Cross of Gold," is an excerpt from William Jennings Bryan's Address to the National Democratic Convention, July 9, 1896, found on http://projects.vassar.edu/1896/crossofgold.html, accessed December 19, 2011.

10 Cited in Jeffrey W. Robbins, "Radical Religion and American Democracy," in Jeffrey W. Robbins and Neal Magee, eds., *The Sleeping Giant has Awoken: The New Politics of Religion in America* (New York: Continuum, 2008), 23.

11 C.B. Macpherson, *The Political Theory of Possessive Individualism* (Oxford: Oxford University Press, 1962).

12 Claude Fischer, *Made in America: A Social History of American Culture and Character* (Chicago: University of Chicago Press, 2010), 40.

13 "Big business and its pursuit of profit, science and its relentless release of energy, politics and its network of influence were all forms of power, and against such institutions Adams saw no authority exists capable of effective resistance." John Patrick Diggins, *The Promise of Pragmatism* (Chicago: University of Chicago Press, 1994), 107.

14 Cited by Fischer, *Made in America*, 102.

15 Michael Kimmage, "The Hands that Built the Conservative Movement," *Dissent* (August 2009), http://www.dissentmagazine.org/online.php?id=281, accessed December 20, 2011.

16 Jedediah Purdy, *A Tolerable Anarchy* (New York: Vintage, 2010), 123.

17 "Among 15 countries providing information to the Luxembourg Income Study, only low-income residents of the United Kingdom are worse off than the poor in the United States.... People at the 10th percentile of the income distribution in the 13 other countries receive higher absolute incomes than a person at the same position of the income distribution in the United States." Gary Burtless and Ron Haskins, "Inequality, Economic Mobility, and Social Policy," in Schuck and Wilson, *Understanding America*, 538.

18 Lawrence Jacobs and Theda Skocpol, eds., *Inequality and American Democracy* (New York: Russell Sage Foundation, 2005); Lisa A. Keister, *Wealth in America: Trends in Wealth Inequality* (New York: Cambridge University Press, 2000); Larry Bartels, *Unequal Democracy: The Political Economy of the New Gilded Age* (Princeton: Princeton University Press, 2008).

19 David Leonhardt, "In Health Bill, Obama Attacks Wealth Inequality," *New York Times*, March 23, 2010, http://www.nytimes.com/2010/03/24/business/24leonhardt.html, accessed December 20, 2011.

20 "The probability that the son of a lowest-quintile father makes it into the highest-quintile group—'rags-to-riches' mobility—is lower in the United States than in all other countries, significantly so for Denmark, Norway and the United Kingdom.... The US appears to be exceptional in having less rather than more upward mobility." Markus Jantti, Knut Roed, Robin Naylor, et al., "American Exceptionalism in a New Light: A Comparison of Intergenerational Earnings Mobility in the Nordic Countries, the United Kingdom and the United States," *IZA Discussion Paper* 1938 (January 2006): 20.

21 Stephen Brooks, *America through Foreign Eyes* (Toronto: Oxford University Press, 2002), 52.

22 Joan Didion, *Where I Was From* (New York: Knopf, 2003), 128.

23 Clinton Rossiter, "The Relevance of Marxism," in *Failure of a Dream? Essays in the History of American Socialism*, ed. John Laslett and Seymour M. Lipset (Garden City: Anchor, 1974), 474.

24 Hodgson, *The Myth of American Exceptionalism*; Archer, *Why Is There No Labor Party in the United States?*, chap. 5.

25 Joyce Appleby, *The Relentless Revolution: A History of Capitalism* (New York: Norton, 2010), 322.

26 Thorstein Veblen, *The Theory of the Leisure Class* (New York: Macmillan, 1912).

27 C. Wright Mills, *The Power Elite* (New York: Oxford University Press, 1956).

28 Appleby, *The Relentless Revolution*, 179.

29 Bartels, *Unequal Democracy*, 149.

30 Cited in Alain Peyrefitte, *Le mal français* (Paris: Plon, 1976), 149–50.

31 Norman W. Taylor, "The French Canadian Industrial Entrepreneur and His Social Environment," in *French Canadian Society*, ed. Marcel Rioux and Yves Martin (Toronto: McClelland and Stewart, 1964), 271–95, 275, 281.

32 Graham D. Taylor, *The Rise of Canadian Business* (Toronto: Oxford University Press, 2009), 28.

33 John Brebner, *North Atlantic Triangle: The Interplay of Canada, the United States and Great Britain* (Toronto: Carleton Library, 1968); Kari Levitt, *Silent Surrender: The Multinational Corporation in Canada* (Toronto: Macmillan, 1970).

34 David Halpern, *The Hidden Wealth of Nations* (Cambridge: Polity, 2010), 152.

35 Richard Wilkinson and Kate Pickett, *The Spirit Level: Why Equality is Better for Everyone* (London: Penguin, 2010).

36 Emmanuel Saez and Michael R. Veall, "The Evolution of High Incomes in Northern America: Lessons from Canadian Evidence," *The American Economic Review* 95, no. 3 (June 2005): 831–49, 839.

37 Enrique Semo, *The History of Capitalism in Mexico: Its Origins, 1521–1763* (Austin: University of Texas Press, 1993), 105.

38 Ross, *El Monstruo*, 60; Earl Shorris, *The Life and Times of Mexico* (New York: Norton, 2004), 544.

39 Ross, *El Monstruo*, 60.

40 Semo, *The History of Capitalism in Mexico*, 157.

41 Fuentes, *A New Time for Mexico*, 38.

42 John Kenneth Turner, *Barbarous Mexico* (1910), excerpted in Jurgen Buchenau, ed., *Mexico Otherwise: Modern Mexico in the Eyes of Foreign Observers* (Albuquerque: University of New Mexico Press, 2005).

43 Paz, *The Labyrinth of Solitude*, 181.

44 Roderic Ai Camp, *Mexico's Mandarins: Crafting a Power Elite for the 21st Century* (Berkeley: University of California Press, 2002), 113, 177.

45 John Gibler, *Mexico Unconquered: Chronicles of Power and Revolt* (San Francisco: City Lights, 2009), 94, 99.

46 Riding, *Mexico*, 221.

47 Leonardo Curzio, "La Transicion a la Democracia y la Construccion de Ciudadania en México," in *La democracia en América Latina, Un Barco a la Deriva*, ed. Waldo Ansaldi (Buenos Aires: FCE, 2006), 328.

48 Curzio, "La Transicion a la Democracia," 329.

49 BBC, "Free Market Flawed, Says Survey," November 9, 2009. In this survey, close to 40 per cent of Mexican respondents agreed with the statement that free market capitalism is fatally flawed and a different economic system is needed as

opposed to 20 per cent or less of Canadian and American respondents agreeing with the statement. http://news.bbc.co.uk/2/hi/in_depth/8347409.stm, accessed May 20, 2011.

50 S. Mainwaring, T. Scully, and Jorge Cullell, "Measuring Success in Democratic Governance," in Scott Mainwaring and Timothy Scully, eds., *Democratic Governance in Latin America* (Stanford: Stanford University Press, 2010), 24.

51 George Grayson, *Mexican Messiah: Andrés Manuel Lopez Obrador* (University Park: Pennsylvania State University Press, 2007), 284.

52 David Lida, *First Stop in the New World: Mexico City, the Capital of the 21st Century* (New York: Penguin, 2009).

SEVEN

Democracy and Its Discontents

"Sail, sail thy best, ship of Democracy,
Not of the Western continent alone,
Earth's resumé entire floats on thy keel
O ship, is steadied by thy spars."
—Walt Whitman,
Thou Mother with Thy Equal Brood[1]

The European settlement of the New World occurred in a non-democratic age. Absolutism reigned in most European courts, and where representative institutions existed, as in Britain, suffrage was greatly limited and politics an affair for the aristocracy and the gentry.

In New Spain, the viceroys were directly responsible to Madrid, with little direct input from the Creoles, let alone the indigenous population. In New France, as well, representative institutions were lacking. But in New England and the other English colonies along the Atlantic seaboard, assemblies with a significant degree of influence over local matters were established. At the same time, various of the Protestant denominations that dotted the religious landscape— for example, Congregationalists and Quakers—provided significant scope for grassroots participation in church government.

Revolution brought its own upheavals. Although the American Revolution was, in Madison's words, "a gentle revolution to end all revolutions,"[2] one which, unlike the French Revolution, did not unleash major social and economic transformations, it proved difficult to keep the democratic impulse entirely in check. True, the framers of the American Constitution were no friends of the term "democracy" and were quite insistent on infusing checks and balances on popular impulses through such devices as an indirectly elected Senate, the Electoral College, and a Supreme Court.[3] Still, the opening words of the American Constitution evoke "We the people," and a progressive extension of popular control over governmental institutions occurred as subsequent decades unfolded.

The Jeffersonian camp, in particular, proved more friendly to popular impulses than its Whig opponents, as did the Jacksonians in their turn. By the time of the Civil War, Lincoln defined the American system of government in words that have become canonical as "government of the people, by the people, and for the people."

Flies in the ointment were there from the beginning. Slavery in the southern states ensured that representative government was a matter only for white slaveholders and their poorer white fellow citizens. The abolition of slavery after 1863 did not remove the stain that characterized race relations in the United States, as Jim Crow laws and segregation remained the norm into the mid-twentieth century. A series of steps—from integration of the armed forces during World War II to the school desegregation decision of the Supreme Court in 1954 to the Civil Rights Act of 1964—began to undo the damage, spurred on by the mobilization of the Civil Rights movement of the 1950s and 1960s. Indigenous peoples were also not part of the democratic equation, as they were confined to having "limited sovereignty" on reserves. Nor were women full and equal members of the American political system until the extension of the franchise in 1919. High abstention rates in elections, as early as the 1920s, underlined a pervasive lack of civic engagement in the American political system.[4]

Nonetheless, seen from the vantage point of the Old World or of the Spanish or Portuguese possessions in the New, the United States and its political system became the harbinger of "a new birth of freedom."[5] It may not have been democracy as the ancients would have understood it, that is, direct rule by the people. It may have subordinated popular input to elite and propertied interests. But it reinvented the notion of democratic government on a new representative basis and with a far more extensive territorial basis than any democracy or republic of the past.

The American model was one that Latin American revolutionaries of the 1810s and 1820s sought to emulate, though with little success. As Jefferson observed in an 1818 letter to John Adams, "While the peoples of the south will succeed against Spain...the dangerous enemy is within their own breasts. Ignorance and superstition will chain their minds under religious and military despotism."[6] As José Victorino Lastarria, a nineteenth-century Chilean historian, noted, "In the North, the people were sovereign in fact and in law, and made the law and administered their interests by means of their representatives. In Spanish America, the people did not exist, society was of no consequence; here the people lived only for the glory and benefit of their sovereign, an absolute and natural master."[7]

The political elites of Britain's remaining North American colonies after 1783 did not take kindly to American notions of republicanism or popular rule. They lent strong support to the idea of a mixed constitution—monarchy, appointed upper house, elected lower house—derived on the prevailing British model. They believed in a more ordered, hierarchical system of government, which they termed British liberties rather than American. By the middle of the nineteenth century, in the aftermath of the failed 1837–38 rebellions in Lower and Upper Canada (Quebec and Ontario), the Canadian colonials had acquired their own version of responsible government. But the path to Canadian political nationality, culminating in the British North America Act of 1867, was an evolutionary, not a revolutionary, one. And it took many further steps for Canada to cut its ties to Britain and its empire.

The Canadian Fathers of Confederation, meeting in the mid-1860s, had little sympathy for republican or democratic principles. For Georges-Étienne Cartier, the leading Quebec figure in the pre-Confederation debates, "The distinction between ourselves and our neighbours was just this: in our federation the monarchical principle would be the leading feature, while on the other side of the line, the ruling power was the will of the mob, the rule of the populace."[8] For Darcy McGee, "We run the risk of being swallowed up by the spirit of universal democracy that prevails in the United States."[9] And for Richard Cartwright, "I own frankly I prefer British liberty to American equality."[10] Is it surprising that there is not a single reference to "the people" in the Constitution Act 1867? The basis of Canadian sovereignty did not formally lie there.

In practice, Canada evolved in an increasingly democratic direction, for much the same reasons democracy had taken root in the United States—a lack of feudal traditions, a heritage of representative institutions and of judicial independence, and a rough equality of condition on the agrarian frontier in particular. So although the form of the Canadian Constitution harked back to principles that were only obliquely democratic, the substance bespoke the same principles of broadening suffrage and parliamentary supremacy that characterized Britain.

In one area, an important one, Canada could claim superiority to the United States as the ultimate repository of universal democratic values. As the terminus of the Underground Railway for blacks fleeing slavery in the pre-Civil War period, Canada (or the colonies that preceded Confederation) was a veritable beacon of liberty. In the words of Joseph Taper, an escaped slave who settled on a farm in St. Catharines, Ontario, "I am now in the land of liberty.... Since I have been in the Queen's dominions I have been well contented. Man is as God intended he should be. That is, all are born free and equal. This is a wholesome law, not like the Southern laws which puts man made in the image of God on level with brutes..."[11]

What was novel about democratic practice in North America? The Americans, without a doubt, carried innovation furthest. They replaced appointed senators with elected ones by the beginning of the twentieth century, reduced the Electoral College to a largely vestigial role, provided for recall and citizen initiatives in roughly half of the American states, and fostered mass popular movements of all kinds. While one can find much to criticize in the workings of the American system—for example, the power of money and vested interests, the blocking role of lobby groups, the demagogic role of sections of the media, and a notable overrepresentation of the middle and upper classes both in registration and turn-out—an indelible feature remains. Messy and inchoate though it may appear and subject to its shares of abuses both at home and abroad, the American system has served as the model of democratic empowerment for many around the world.

Slavery was eventually overcome as the result of a bloody civil war. The Gilded Age gave way to a period of progressive reform. The crisis of 1929 gave rise to the experimentation of the New Deal. A century of Jim Crow laws was swept aside with the 1954 Supreme Court desegregation decision and with the Civil Rights Act of 1964. Hawkish stances in foreign policy have been balanced by a more temperate view of American power in a multipolar world. The American system has an inherent ability to correct *some* of its self-inflicted wounds and move on while retaining its core political institutions intact.

At the same time, the separation of powers introduced rigidity into the operation of government. Administrations can propose, and Congressional committees dispose; the courts can temper government initiatives, even in times of crisis like that of the Great Depression of the 1930s. The frequency of elections introduces its own constraints on what politicians are willing to support. Populist initiatives, for their part, can stymie the taxing capacity of governments and set the stage for near-bankruptcy by default in states such as California. It can lead to the near-paralysis of the political system, as the emergence of the Tea Party and the 2011 crisis over the American debt ceiling has underlined. And money can weigh heavily on a political system, where well-heeled interests can easily out-balance all others.[12] So the American system of government can be as much a symbol of dysfunction as of democratic apotheosis.

Does Canada do better by this standard? Yes, if one is looking for governmental efficacy, since the British-derived system of a fusion of executive and legislative powers provides for the ability of governments with parliamentary or legislative majorities to act more effectively than their American counterparts. The danger here, however, lies in potential abuse when the same political party stays in power through numerous elections and when political leaders, as has not been uncommon at both the federal and provincial level, occupy office for long stretches of time. The result is a system of strong-man prime ministers or premiers—Maurice Duplessis in Quebec, W.A.C. Bennett in British Columbia, William Aberhardt in Alberta, Mitch Hepburn in Ontario, and Joey Smallwood in Newfoundland, to name a few—subject only to the restraints that the courts or occasionally the media are able to provide. Populist input in Canada, the western provinces aside, has been weaker than in the United States. And the influence of big money, while somewhat more restrained than in the United States, is also a recurring issue in Canada.[13]

The Canadian temper of government has been more top-down than bottom-up. Canada has not been noted for democratic innovation and is characterized more by deference to authority than by a healthy questioning of the use of governmental power. This has begun to shift somewhat with the coming of the Charter of Rights and Freedoms and greater recourse to the courts to deal with contentious public policy questions, e.g., Aboriginal rights, gay rights, and gender rights. Canada and its provinces have also witnessed a more frequent use of referenda on such contentious questions as Quebec sovereignty, constitutional change (the Charlottetown Accord), electoral reform, and the harmonized sales tax (HST) in British Columbia in 2011. Commissions of inquiry provide some amends for past misuses of power, for instance, the Gomery inquiry into the sponsorship scandal during the prime ministership of Liberal Jean Chrétien and the Braidwood inquiry into the taser death of Robert Dziekanski at the hands of the RCMP in the Vancouver airport in 2007.

The current Conservative government has centralized powers in the hands of the prime minister to a greater degree than ever. It has abused the power of proroguing Parliament on two occasions in recent years. And it has shown scant concern for the civil liberties of Canadians, be it protesters at the G-20 summit in Toronto in June 2010 or the imprisonment abroad of Canadian citizens such as Omar Khadr, held at Guantanamo since 2005. The Canadian electoral system, moreover, with its first-past-the-post character, systematically penalizes third parties without a strong regional base and overcompensates dominant parties at the expense of their rivals. Germany, for one, with its mixed single member/proportional representation system, has a far fairer electoral system than does Canada.

Of the three North American states, Mexico is the one where democracy has been a particularly fragile bloom. After Independence, Mexico experienced ten military coups within the first 30 years; one of Latin America's most notorious dictators, Porfirio Díaz, in power for 35 years to 1911; and a one-party system, the legacy of the Mexican Revolution, as the norm until 2000. The root of the problem was that civil society was weak in Mexico from the beginning. As Claudio Lomnitz notes "the peasant sector and popular sector had no sacrosanct private sphere from which to criticize the state, and therefore no protected basis for liberal citizenship."[14] As the French political scientist André Siegfried earlier observed, "Never have I heard so much talk about Constitutions as in those countries where the constitution is violated every day.... The law has majesty only in words."[15]

The priorities of the Mexican Revolution were instituting agrarian reform and labour laws, gaining national control over resources, and limiting the power of the Church—not in democratic reforms per se.[16] A series of strong presidents perpetuated the top-down authoritarian traditions inherited from the colonial period. As Villegas observed in the early 1950s, "the men of the revolution were magnificent destroyers, but nothing they created to replace what was destroyed has turned out to be indisputably better." The result was a "six-yearly absolute monarchy" rather than a pluralistic democracy.[17]

Extra-parliamentary movements were a recurring phenomenon. The *Cristeros* rebellion of the late 1920s was a reaction from traditionally Catholic parts of the country to the heavy-handed attempts by governments such as that of President Calleo to impose secularism at any cost. The student rebellion of 1968, paralleling a similar wave of rebellions in Europe, the United States, and Canada, spoke to multiple frustrations with a closed and repressive political system. The Zapatista Rebellion in Chiapas, beginning January 1, 1994, brought to a head the alienation of Mexico's indigenous peoples and their ongoing economic deprivation.

Mario Vargas-Llosa once described Mexico's long-ruling party, the PRI, as "a perfect dictatorship."[18] Opposition parties were allowed legal existence and limited representation in Congress and state legislatures, but fraud was widespread, and any serious challenge to the existing order, such as Cuauhténoc Cárdenas's presidential bid of 1988, was stymied by every available means.

Andrew Reading, an informed American student of Mexican politics, described some of the practices in the 1988 election: public access to vote-tallying computers on election night 1988 was shut off; tens of thousands of Cárdenas ballots were burned in smoldering heaps along roadsides and stuffed in dumpsters; and tally sheets were altered by the addition of zeros in the PRI columns. An independent statistical analysis of the data suggests Cárdenas won the election with 41 to 42 per cent of the vote to Salinas at 36 per cent and the PAN (the centre-right National Action Party) candidate at 22 per cent.[19] It was another 12 years before Mexico experienced a change in political parties at the centre, with the election of Vincente Fox of PAN to the presidency. Subsequently, accusations of fraud surrounded the closely contested presidential election of 2006, which saw Felipe Calderón just edging out Manuel Obrador.

Mexican politics has become more open and pluralistic over the past two decades. NAFTA may well be one reason as Mexican electoral procedures have come under greater outside scrutiny than before. But as Guillermo O'Donnell, a leading contemporary expert on Latin America, notes, "Ours are democracies of truncated or low intensity citizenship."[20] For the independent Mexico City newspaper, *La Jornada,* commenting on the 60 per cent abstention rate in the 2003 mid-term elections, Mexico is "a democracy without people." For Enrique Pedrero, former senator, governor of Tabasco, and chair of the faculty of political science at the National Autonomous University of Mexico, "the full democratic reordering of Mexico requires citizens."[21] For Jorge Alonso, "The roots of electoral democracy are not deep.... The greatest failure lies in the absence of social rights, and in access to social welfare."[22] And that is without reckoning with the deep scars that narco-trafficking has inflicted on Mexico's democratic transition and political system, especially in its northern cities and states.[23]

How should one assess the state of democracy in North America today? Some of the critiques that have been applied to the Mexican regime can be applied to all three North American countries. There has been a decline of citizen participation, as measured by turn-out in elections at both the federal and provincial/state levels in Canada and the United States. Ordinary citizens have a sense of limited efficacy when it comes to being able to influence government policies. Globalization has resulted in the displacement of jobs, especially in the industrial sector, and the crises that have rocked the international financial system in the wake of the derivatives-induced meltdown of 2007–08 have underlined the limits on economic decision-making by individual nation-states. All this spells trouble for the prevailing model of democracy based on representative institutions within the nation-state.

Pierre Rosanvallon has suggested that "Democracy is concurrently and simultaneously an order of civic activity, a regime, a form of society, and a mode of government."[24] As a consequence, there is a serious deficiency when civic activity declines or when the sense of social cohesion is frayed. Nor is it simply the case that one can displace one's hopes for resolution onto transnational institutions. The European Union has proven to be flat-footed in dealing with the fiscal crises faced by some of its weakest members (that is, Greece, Ireland, and Portugal). The G-8 and G-20 represent useful forums for discussion among leading economic powers, but they have no legitimacy to enforce their decisions. Nor can the UN be seen as an instrument of democratic governance at the international level. It elicits little of the loyalty that nation-states, democratic or not, can demand from their own citizens and suffers from a distinct deficiency of both efficacy and resources.

Domestically, reconciling democracy in the political arena with the structural inequality that characterizes relations in the economic sphere remains an ongoing problem. Bill Moyers has observed that "Plutocracy and democracy don't mix. Plutocracy too long tolerated leaves democracy on the auction block, subject to the highest bidder."[25] Sheldon Wolin, a leading American writer on democratic theory, has noted that "Managed democracy is centred on containing electoral politics; it is cool, even hostile toward social democracy beyond promoting literacy, job training."[26] Richard Wilkinson and Kate Pickett have underlined the negative impact of inequality for the quality of life of ordinary citizens in contemporary Western societies, with the United States, despite its high aggregate GDP, scoring toward the very bottom of the comparative indices.[27] Perhaps satiated liberal democracies, with possessive individualism as a dominant value, are bad for democratic empowerment. Democracy is not only about constitutional constraints on rulers, periodic elections, or functioning multi-party systems—it entails a measure of genuine economic and social equality, if the demos is not to be reduced to a strictly ancillary role in the political system that bears its name.

All this suggests the need for modesty, not triumphalism, in our understanding of how democracy in the North American context operates. Large conglomerates such as Televisa in Mexico, Fox News in the United States, or Postmedia in Canada have a disproportionate degree of influence in shaping public opinion. Major donors to political parties—oil companies, financial institutions, and utilities, among others—carry disproportionate weight when it comes to decision-making that affects their interests. Short-term concerns and private interests tend to prevail over long-term and public ones. Minority groups, such as indigenous peoples or blacks, are usually at the short end of the stick when it comes to income, employment, or living conditions. Far from there being a shared North American community, there are legitimate doubts about the strength of shared community and civic values within each of the three North American states. It is not only in the Old World that democracy has so often been beleaguered or suppressed. The New World has fallen short of living up to democracy's highest ideals as well.

Notes

1 Walt Whitman, "Thou Mother with Thy Equal Brood," in Whitman, *Complete Poetry and Collected Prose*, 570.

2 Cited in Michael Kammen, *A Season of Youth: The American Revolution and the Historical Imagination* (New York: Knopf, 1978), 212.

3 Cf. Edmund Morgan, *Inventing the People* (New York: Norton, 1988), 173, contrasting the fiction of an invincible yeoman as opposed to the deeply entrenched social hierarchy that dominated the post-revolutionary United States.

4 Cf. an editorial in the *Los Angeles Times* as early as August 2, 1924 bemoaning a 50 per cent turn-out rate in elections by sixth- or seventh-generation Americans; cited in Fischer, *Made in America*, 187.

5 Abraham Lincoln, "The Gettysburg Address," http://showcase.netins.net/web/creative/lincoln/speeches/gettysburg.htm, accessed December 20, 2011.

6 Tucker and Hendrickson, *Empire of Liberty*, 253.

7 Leopoldo Zea, *The Latin American Mind* (Norman: University of Oklahoma Press, 1963), 78–79.

8 Janet Ajzenstat et al., eds., *Canada's Founding Debates* (Toronto: University of Toronto Press, 2003), 185.

9 Ajzenstat et al., *Canada's Founding Debates*, 188.

10 Ajzenstat et al., *Canada's Founding Debates*, 19.

11 Cited in Howe, *What Hath God Wrought*, 266.

12 A good example is the multi-billionaire Koch brothers, who have funneled more than $100 million into dozens of political organizations, trying to steer the United States in a more libertarian direction. Cf. National Public Radio, "The Brothers Koch: Rich, Political and Playing to Win" (August 26, 2010), http://www.npr.org/templates/story/story/php?storyID=129425186, accessed May 20, 2011.

13 Major political corruption cases over time include the CPR, Beauharnois, sponsorship, and BC Rail scandals.

14 Lomnitz, *Deep Mexico*, 75.

15 André Siegfried, *Amérique Latine*, 100, cited in Ramos, *Profile of Man and Culture in Mexico*, 48.

16 "Mexico has never been ready for political democracy. It is not ready for such a democracy at present," Tannenbaum, *Peace by Revolution*, 151.

17 "To create in Mexico a democracy with some aspects of authenticity...would discourage any sensitive man.... A country whose population is scattered into an infinity of tiny settlements in which civic life is at present impossible, settlements which live isolated from one another, out of the reach of knowledge and of wealth—such a country cannot suddenly create a favourable environment for conscientious and responsible civic life." Daniel Cosío Villegas, "Mexico's Crisis," in Gilbert Joseph and Timothy Henderson, eds., *The Mexico Reader: History, Culture, Politics* (Durham: Duke University Press, 2002), 472.

18 Cited in Ross, *El Monstruo*, 338.

19 Andrew Reading, "Chiápas is Mexico: The Imperative of Political Reform," *World Policy Journal* 11, no. 1 (1994): 20.

20 Guillermo O'Donnell, cited in Lawrence Whitehead, *Latin America: A New Interpretation* (London: Palgrave Macmillan, 2006): 209.

21 Pedrero, *La cuerda tenso*, 307.

22 Jorge Alonso, "Democracia y Nuevos Municipios," in *La remunicipalizacion de Chiapas*, ed. X.L. Solano and A.B. Cal y Mayor (Mexico: Porrua, 2007).

23 "The illegal drug trade does not only affect the law-enforcement capacities of the state and the political regime. By undermining the rule of law and democratic accountability, fostering 'militarization,' and provoking human rights violations, this business challenges the alleged democratic nature of recent political change in Mexico." José Luis Velasco, *Insurgency, Authoritarianism, and Drug Trafficking in Mexico's "Democratization"* (New York: Routledge, 2005).

24 Pierre Rosanvallon, *La légitimité démocratique* (Paris: Seuil, 2008).

25 Bill Moyers, "Welcome to the Plutocracy!," speech in the Howard Zinn Lecture Series, Boston University, October 29, 2010; see Wednesday 3 November 2010

truthout: http://archive.truthout.org/bill-moyers-money-fights-hard-and-it-fights-dirty64766, accessed December 22, 2011.

26 Sheldon Wolin, *Democracy Incorporated* (Princeton: Princeton University Press, 2008), 47.

27 Wilkinson and Pickett, *The Spirit Level,* 8, 131, 142, 159–61, 174, 183, 190, 239–40.

EIGHT

The Protean State

"The state or the United States."
—*Graham Spry, Canadian broadcasting pioneer*[1]

Canada, the United States, and Mexico are sovereign states. From the perspective of the international system, each can claim legitimate authority over the territory and population that it encompasses. Forms of government and the extent of public administration and policy are matters to be resolved in accordance with national concerns.

There are significant differences in the way state structures have developed in the three countries. While all three have federal systems, in practice the United States began as a fairly decentralized federation, Canada as a fairly centralized one, and Mexico as a country in which the central government, until recently, could run roughshod over its states.

Constitutionally, the United States and Mexico are both republics with a formal division of powers among the executive, legislature, and the courts. This has had palpable significance in the American case, where despite the emergence of a more imperial presidency in the twentieth century, both Congress and the courts have made their powers felt on multiple occasions. In Mexico, on the other hand, until recently the presidency was the dominant institution, with Congress under the control of the same ruling party and the courts an ancillary power.[2] Canada has had a parliamentary form of government modelled on Britain, which has led to a fusion of executive and legislative powers when the ruling party, as is usually the case, has had a parliamentary majority. The courts, on the other hand, have always enjoyed a fair degree of autonomy and have emerged strengthened from the patriation of the Constitution in 1982 with the addition of the Charter of Rights and Freedoms.

Institutional arrangements aside, what about underlying attitudes of the population to governmental authority and to the scope and range of policies that have emerged? Here, the patterns have been strikingly different. The Americans developed a relatively weak state at first, but it has been much strengthened in the century and a half since the Civil War. Canada has had a strong state in the economic and social arena, but it is one whose legitimacy has been challenged on a number of occasions by the forces of Quebec nationalism. And Mexico is a strong state in appearance but a much weaker one when it comes to the ability to tax its citizens and corporations or deliver effective protection or social services to its inhabitants.

In the American case, as Bernard Bailyn has observed, the new country the American revolutionaries set out to build was one where "authority was distrusted and held in constant scrutiny...and where the use of power over the lives of men was jealously guarded and severely restricted."[3] The constituent states had preceded the establishment of a federal government. This put effective limits on how far the federal government could go in flexing its powers, all the more given the deep sectional cleavage between slave and free states. While the federal government was able to act decisively in matters such as the Louisiana Purchase, various Indian Wars, and the Mexican-American War, it was confined to a more limited role in economic matters. Jefferson's reference in his First Inaugural Address of 1801 to the need for economy in public expense spoke to this view.[4]

In the aftermath of the Civil War, the federal government assumed an enhanced authority. Yet during the Gilded Age, its role was far more one of handmaiden to entrepreneurs and corporations, through railway subsidies for instance, than of constituting an active countervailing power of its own.[5] The odd exception, such as the Sherman Antitrust Act of 1890, did not undercut this.

By the first decades of the twentieth century, in the Progressive era, the federal government gained a more effective role through the establishment of the Federal Reserve System and the enactment of a federal income tax, among other measures. More signal changes came in the 1930s with the New Deal. Faced with the near collapse of the capitalist system in the Great Depression, Roosevelt and Congress were prepared to countenance a degree of governmental intervention not experienced before. The National Recovery Act, the Civilian Conservation Corps, the Tennessee Valley Authority, the Wagner Act, and the Social Security Act were key landmarks of the period. But it is worth noting that "[e]ven during the Great Depression, many local officeholders believed that New Deal support programs simply subsidized the indolent and the officials subverted their implementation."[6]

The impulse for reform flagged in the immediate postwar period, one of unheralded American prosperity, but picked up again in the 1960s with legislation such as the Civil Rights Act, Medicaid, and the War on Poverty. And there the compass froze, as the neo-conservative policies of the Reagan Administration and its successors moved increasingly rightwards. A quip by Ronald Reagan sums this up rather well. What, he once asked an audience, were the nine most terrifying words in the English language? "I'm from the government, and I'm here to help."[7] The battle surrounding Barack Obama's health care reform initiative, extending medical coverage to 32 million uninsured Americans, underlines just how resistant large sections of American public opinion have become to increased governmental social expenditures. Only 22 per cent of Americans, according to an April 19, 2010 Reuters survey, trusted their government to do the right thing.[8]

The American state has proven to be more of a Leviathan when it comes to its international role. Despite George Washington's well-known admonition in his Farewell Address for the United States to refrain from involvement in foreign wars, the United States has been engaged in such ventures with growing frequency. The Mexican-American War in the mid-nineteenth century was one; the Spanish-American at the end of that century another, with public opinion swept along by jingoistic sentiments, orchestrated by the Hearst newspaper chain. Both in 1917–18 and again in 1941–45, public opinion strongly backed the war effort, as it did in the Cold War period, which saw the permanent enhancement of the country's military and security apparatus. True, there has been opposition to American operations abroad—Henry Thoreau withheld taxes over what he saw as the unjust Mexican-American War; William James opposed the Spanish-American War; many students opposed the Vietnam War. But, especially since 9/11, the Pentagon, the CIA (Central Intelligence Agency), the FBI (Federal Bureau of Investigation), and Homeland Security have become the most powerful agencies of the federal government. They bolster the imperial role the United States has come to assume in the contemporary world.

There is a tendency in the United States to favour the use of tax write-offs and incentives over direct government expenditure. There is also a strong impetus to look to charitable and philanthropic organizations for educational and cultural programs that in many other countries are funded by government. The United States is the only Western country to have no Ministry of Cultural Affairs or its equivalent; it has a very weak system of public broadcasting—much of it individually financed—when compared to others. Nor does it provide for its poorer citizens in housing, social security, or unemployment insurance in the way that most others do. This too is part of American exceptionalism.

Canada has developed a rather different approach to the use of the state. This did not happen overnight, nor has government always been as capacious or socially inclined as has generally been the case since World War II. In its early phase, the Canadian state, as befits a new and largely unsettled country, was concerned with building infrastructure, such as canals and railways, and fostering immigration, especially from Britain and Western Europe. Canadian governments also introduced high tariffs, as a way of promoting industrial activity and avoiding the fate of "hewers of wood and drawers of water." There were, however, odd examples of direct state ownership, such as the creation of Ontario Hydro in 1906.

World War I brought federal income tax and the move to a more professional, merit-based civil service. The period between the wars saw the coming of means-tested old age pensions and a number of state enterprises, in particular the CBC, the Canada Wheat Board, and Trans-Canada Airlines (later Air Canada).

During World War II the government assumed a commanding role over the industrial and agricultural activities of the country. There were also fledgling moves toward enhanced social security with the establishment of federal responsibility over unemployment insurance through constitutional amendment in 1940 and through the universal family allowance program of 1944.

In 1945, Canada became the first country to embrace Keynesian-type economic policies. Benefitting from its distance from the killing fields both of Europe and Asia and from its resource sector, Canada experienced a lengthy postwar boom, with only occasional interruption in the late 1950s. This period was marked by the enhanced role for government in the social and cultural arenas and with respect to economic policies. Old age pensions became more generous as well as universal in coverage. Free hospitalization was introduced, and in the mid-1960s, building on the Saskatchewan example of 1962, the federal government and other provinces embarked on a government-financed health system known as medicare. The result has been a health system which costs about two-thirds of the American system on a per capita basis and does a far better job of serving the lower income section of the population. Canadian unemployment insurance benefits and welfare allowances were also significantly increased in the 1960s, though they were to be scaled back in later decades.

The Canada Council for the Arts was established in 1957 and became a major purveyor of funds for artists, writers, musicians, theatres, orchestras, and the like. All levels of government came to fund the post-secondary system of education more generously from the 1960s on, leading to increased levels of access to higher education by Canadians.

In its own way, the Quebec government also played a much more interventionist role than previously with the nationalization of the remaining private electricity companies in Quebec in 1962 and in 1965 the establishment of the Quebec Pension Plan (in parallel to the Canada Pension Plan), which provided a significant amount of investment capital to help foster Quebec-run enterprises in the province. In important ways, the state had replaced the Church as the key institution in Quebec, assuming direct responsibility for education and social programs that had been delegated previously. A heady new strain of Quebec nationalism was in the air to power this transition, culminating in the emergence of a separatist party, the Parti Québécois. This party gained power on four occasions after 1976 and initiated two referenda on the question of sovereignty (or more precisely, sovereignty-association and sovereignty-partnership). The first, in 1980, resulted in 40.5 per cent of the electorate voting in favour; the second, in 1995, came much closer to a win for the sovereignty cause, garnering 49.4 per cent of the popular vote.

The 1980s were characterized by a swing away from a strong role for the state in Canada. Neo-conservatism had its supporters in Canada, and a number of state corporations such as Air Canada, the CNR, and Saskatchewan Potash were privatized. State expenditures, both federal and provincial, were reduced in the 1990s. Yet, the figures for overall social expenditure in Canada at 19 per cent have remained significantly higher than those for the United States at 12 per cent, not to speak of Mexico at 2 per cent.[9] The overall Canadian attitude to the role of government has proven more enduringly positive than that of Americans.

One reason for this lies in the existence of a socialist strain in Canadian politics largely absent in the United States. Though the Cooperative Commonwealth Federation (CCF), founded in 1933, and its successor the New Democratic Party (NDP), founded in 1961, have never held power federally, the latter has at times held the balance of power in minority parliaments. It has formed governments, at different times, in five of Canada's provinces and has been the Official Opposition in Ottawa since the May 2011 election. The Parti Québécois, its sovereignty stance aside, has often had a social democratic orientation when it has been in office. The Bloc Québécois has had a similar policy orientation at the federal level.

The Liberal Party of Canada, the governing party of Canada for most of the twentieth century, has harboured both business-oriented and more socially oriented wings. Almost all of the important federal programs that have led to the development of a Canadian welfare state were enacted by Liberal governments at different points, most especially by that of Lester Pearson in the 1960s.

For 60 years, the conservative party in Canada was called the Progressive Conservative Party; this changed in 2003 when the party merged with the western-based Canadian Reform Conservative Alliance to become simply the Conservative Party of Canada. The "Red Tory" tradition made earlier Progressive Conservative governments at the federal level open to significant state intervention in the economy.[10] And provincial Progressive Conservative governments, such as those of John Robarts and Bill Davis in Ontario, were no less prepared to introduce timely social programs than their Liberal or NDP counterparts. This is a lot less true of the current Conservative Party and government, which have a more strongly market orientation.

A second factor at play was the strong British influence that pervaded Canadian politics down to World War II. Britain's establishment of a state-funded broadcasting system in 1926 legitimized a similar move to establish the CBC in the 1930s. To the degree that the Beveridge Plan of 1942 laid the foundation for enhanced social security in postwar Britain, it also helped to further the process in Canada, albeit with some delay. The French social security system may also have had some resonance for Quebec in the period after 1960. Overall, Canada may well have been more prone to greater European influence in this area of policy than the United States.

One further factor needs to be highlighted, and that is the crucial role of nationalism. Policies pursued by successive Canadian governments, such as railway building, can be explained as defensive measures aimed at warding off an expansionist United States by consolidating east–west ties.[11] Canadian governments were aware of the lure of the United States, and initiatives such as the National Policy, the National Energy Board, and the Foreign Investment Review Agency spoke to this concern. Canadians were prepared to support state-run electricity corporations, railways, airlines, broadcasting corporations, and the like as legitimate tools for nation- or province-building. So while Ronald Reagan enhanced his political support by deriding the role of government, Pierre Trudeau countered this, on the occasion of Reagan's state visit to Canada in March 1981, with the observation that "Here in Canada, our own realities have sometimes made it necessary for governments to further enterprise. Those realities and that necessity are still with us today."[12] This stance has been weakened in the 30 years that have followed; neo-conservative policies are in the ascendancy in various provinces, and successive federal governments have been prepared to privatize Crown enterprises and prune government expenditures. Still, state expenditures as a share of total GDP have remained higher than in the United States, and the overall Canadian attitude toward redistributive programs is more positive than that of Americans.

Mexico is a different story altogether. The post-independence Mexican state was a very weak one. Attempts were made in the 1850s to reform it in a liberal direction, but this was stymied by the Díaz dictatorship, which under the gloss of economic development held the country under its repressive sway from 1876 to 1911. The chaos of the Mexican Revolution gave way to a strongly centralized state under the domination of a catch-all political party, the PRI, and a succession of presidents, held to a single six-year term by the 1917 Constitution. Their policies varied widely, from strongly nationalist and anti-clerical in the 1920s, to socially progressive and interventionist in the 1930s, to increasingly market-friendly in more recent decades.

Intellectuals such as Carlos Fuentes have welcomed the all-pervasive character of the Mexican state in preserving Mexican independence,[13] even while others such as Octavio Paz came to deride "the philanthropic ogre."[14] For Leopoldo, writing in an earlier period, "To expect everything from the State—this is indeed one of the greatest evils inherited from Spain."[15] For Samuel Ramos, "The State is omnipotent...the character of their citizens is weak."[16] For Roberto Bolaño, in his apocalyptical novel, *2666*, "In Mexico intellectuals work for the state. It was like that under the PRI and it'll be the same under the PAN. The intellectual himself may be a passionate defender of the state or a critic. The state doesn't care. The state feeds him and watches over him in silence."[17]

More to the point is the relative weakness of Mexican governments in comparison to the role of governments in Canada or the United States when it comes to delivering services to the population. Corruption is rampant. As Alan Riding describes it, "After the Revolution, most generals were bought off with expropriated haciendas, while [President] Obregón himself used to boast: 'There is no general who can resist a cannonade of 50,000 pesos.'"

In the postwar period, "the most visible form of official corruption, *la mor-dida*—the bite of the traffic police—is almost part of the way of life, and it takes place thousands of times daily.... The corruption of the Mexican press was also legendary, with monthly stipends—*el embute*—for favoured reporters. Student protest marchers referred to it as *Prensa Vendida* or Sold-Out Press."[18]

An inability to generate sufficient tax revenues is another ongoing concern. The central government is all too dependent on Petroléos Mexicanos (PEMEX) for its revenue, in the process denying the company much needed capital for exploration and development.[19] Tax evasion is common. The Mexican government received only 11 per cent of GDP in tax revenue, one of the poorest records for Latin American countries.[20]

Not surprisingly, millions of Mexicans working in the informal sector of the economy lack stable jobs, trade union organizations, and any kind of health care or pension coverage. Mexico is near the very bottom of OECD countries when it comes to social security expenditure. The *Oportunidades* program, providing modest allowances to families whose children attend school, is a mere pittance in the larger picture of income inequality. Rather than a welfare state, it is more accurate to describe Mexico as an ill-fare state[21] for a significant part of its population.

What is perhaps most lacking in Mexico is a culture of citizenship. The top-down role of the state is sometimes referred to as *aztequismo,* something inherited from the Aztecs via the no less top-down structure of authority in New Spain under the Spanish viceroys. The 35 years of dictatorship by Porfirio Díaz left its mark, as did the one-party domination of the PRI through the successive administrations of its twentieth-century presidents.

Mexican governments have often used nationalism as a device to ensure their legitimacy—not unlike the case with Canadian and Quebec governments. When he was the Minister for Education in the 1920s, José Vasconcelos promoted Mexican national identity through a centrally controlled education system and through sponsoring the mural paintings of Rivera and others.[22] Lázaro Cardénas, Mexico's most progressive president, nationalized the foreign-controlled petroleum industry in 1938 with the slogan *El petróleo es nuestro* ("The petroleum is ours"). A collection was established to help raise the $350 million to pay off the oil barons, with Mexicans from all walks of life—from wealthy matrons to prisoners in the Morelia penitentiary—contributing what they could to the national effort.[23] The construction of the National Museum of Anthropology in Chapultepec Park in Mexico City, housing many of the pre-Columbian archaeological treasures of the country, is another example of the government's promotion of nationalism. In foreign policy as well, Mexican presidents often tried to ensure a degree of distance from American foreign policy, for instance by maintaining ongoing relations with Cuba after its 1959 Revolution or, like Canada, by not supporting the American-led invasion of Iraq in 2003. As the old quip about the PRI has it, "the government runs its foreign policy with its left hand, and it runs its domestic politics with its right hand."

The right hand certainly prevailed in the postwar period when President Alemán welcomed American capital with open arms. This was followed by a succession of presidents who bowed to capitalist pressures: "President Miguel de la Madrid privatized more than 900 of the 1,600 state-owned enterprises between 1982 and 1988; Carlos Salinas sold off 300 of the remaining state firms by 1994, including the telecommunications giant TelMex to Carlos Slim."[24] NAFTA has further integrated the Mexican economy with that of its North American partners, ensuring that a more market-oriented approach will follow. The replacement of PRI by PAN in the presidency in 2000 in no way altered this. Vincente Fox, after all, had earlier served as president of Coca Cola Mexico, and Felipe Calderón, unlike his fire-breathing opponent Manuel Obrador in the 2006 election, was equally pro-business in his inclinations.

The role of the state is a major distinguishing characteristic among the three North American countries. The Canadian case, especially since World War II, has been one of a mixed economy, with government providing significant social services such as medicare through a redistributive tax system. Overall, Canadian expenditures on a per capita basis constitute the highest for the three countries; levels of inequality are the lowest; longevity and access to health services for all sections of society are the best; and the educational performance of its students is superior when measured by competitive international exams.

The United States, on the other hand, with a government sector responsible for a good deal of economic activity, is considerably less organized and efficient in this regard than Canada or the northern European states. It has some of the characteristics of what James Galbraith has termed a predator state, falling victim to private interests who encroach on the public purposes of government activities to their own advantage.[25] It has among the highest levels of income inequality for OECD countries, compounded by the super-profits earned by the top 1 per cent and top 0.1 per cent of income earners over the past 30 years since the so-called Reagan Revolution began. As a consequence, it has proven much less generous in providing for the needs of its poorer citizens than Canada. (Income inequality has also increased in Canada, as noted in Chapter 6, but taxes and programs have not been cut as drastically as in the United States.)

The real challenge for Mexico over the coming decades is not that of diminishing the role played by the state so much as ensuring a degree of efficacy in state interventions. The failure of the Mexican government to provide effective leadership after the earthquake in Mexico City of 1985 is an example of where the system falls down (not that the Bush Administration in the United States did any better when the Hurricane Katrina disaster hit New Orleans). An inability to end the narco-terror that is wreaking havoc in many of Mexico's northern and western states is another. An inability to get the rich to pay their fair share of taxes is yet a third (this is something Mexico shares with its American neighbour). The state may be the rampart of Mexican national identity, but it has yet to prove effective when it comes to providing essential protections, economic opportunities, and services to its burgeoning population.

One further observation: the existence of sovereign states is the greatest single obstacle to the possibility of political integration at the North American level. Membership in international organizations such as the UN and its associated specialized agencies, in regional bodies such as the Organization of American States, or in trade associations such as NAFTA is one thing; a willingness to cede major power to supra-national bodies quite another. Citizenship still flows through membership in the nation-state, and the loyalty of citizens, their sense of constituting a community of shared destiny, cannot be easily extended beyond this. Some of the problems that the European Union is currently experiencing flow from this fact. For while citizens may be willing to make major sacrifices for their fellow citizens and even lay down their lives when their nation-states call on them to do so, they are much less inclined to do the same for something as abstract as a continent. Here, the twenty-first century, despite cosmopolitan and globalizing currents that transcend the nation-state, is unlikely to prove all that different from the twentieth or the nineteenth.

Notes

1 Graham Spry (of the Canadian Radio League) in Canada, House of Commons, 1932, Special Committee on Radio Broadcasting: Minutes and Proceedings of Evidence (Ottawa: F.A. Aclaud, 1932), 43.

2 "[T]he highest court in the land was only a sham power." Enrique Krauze, *Mexico: Biography of Power* (New York: Harper Collins, 1997), 568.

3   Bernard Bailyn, *The Ideological Origins of the American Revolution* (Cambridge, MA: Harvard University Press, 1967), 319.

4. "Economy in the public expence, that labor may be lightly burthened." Thomas Jefferson, First Inaugural Address, March 4, 1801, http://www.bartleby.com/124/pres16.html, accessed December 20, 2011.

5   Cf. the scathing editorial in the *New York Times* in February 1867 entitled "The Tyranny of Corporations," arguing that "Every public means of transit is in the hands of the tyrants of modern society—the capitalists.... Even the State Legislatures can barely hold their own against these powerful monopolies. They can bribe and bully and cajole, so as to squelch any bill directed against them." Cited in T.J. Stiles, *The First Tycoon: The Epic Life of Cornelius Vanderbilt* (New York: Knopf, 2009), 444.

6   Fischer, *Made in America*, 53.

7   Ronald Reagan, quoted in the *Economist,* "Onwards and Upwards" (December 19, 2009): 40.

8   *Reuters,* "Majority of Americans distrust the government," April 19, 2010, citing a Pew Research Center survey, http://www.reuters.com/article/2010/04/19/us-americans-government-poll-idUSTRE63I0FB20100419, accessed May 20, 2011.

9   Wil C. Pansters, ed., *Citizens of the Pyramid: Essays on Mexican Political Culture* (Amsterdam: Thela, 1997), 185.

10 For the classic argument on this subject, see Gad Horowitz, "Conservatism, Liberalism, and Socialism in Canada: An Interpretation," *Canadian Journal of Economics and Political Science* 32, no. 1 (1966): 143–71.

11 Hugh Aitken, "Defensive Expansionism: The State and Economic Growth in Canada," in *Approaches to Canadian Economic History,* ed. W.T. Easterbrook and Mel Watkins (Toronto: Carleton Library, 1967), 183–221.

12 Pierre Trudeau, 32nd Parliament Special Session, *Hansard,* March 11, 1981.

13 Carlos Fuentes, in Maarten von Delden, *Carlos Fuentes, Mexico and Modernity* (Nashville: Vanderbilt University Press, 1993), 123.

14 Octavio Paz, *El ogro filantrópico* (Barcelona: Seix Barral, 1979).

15 Zea, *The Latin American Mind,* 80.

16 Ramos, *Profile of Man and Culture in Mexico,* 49.

17 Roberto Bolaño, *2666* (New York: Farrar, Straus and Giroux, 2008), 121.

18 Riding, *Mexico,* 120, 122, 130–31.

19 Sidney Weintraub, *Unequal Partners: The United States and Mexico* (Pittsburgh: University of Pittsburgh Press, 2010), 13.

20 Evelyn Huber and John Stephens, "Successful Social Policy Regimes?," in Mainwaring and Scully, 201.

21 "Policymakers at the Economic Commission for Latin America and the Caribbean meetings in the first decade of the twenty-first century referred to the state

in Latin America not as a welfare state but as an 'ill fare state.'" Alejandro Foxley, "More Market or More State for Latin America?" in Mainwaring and Scully,
Democratic Governance in Latin America, 130.

22 Funes, *Salvar la nacion*, 116.

23 Ross, *El Monstruo*, 183–84.

24 Gibler, *Mexico Unconquered*, 274.

25 James Galbraith, *The Predator State: How Conservatives Abandoned the Market
and Why Liberals Should Too* (New York: The Free Press, 2008).

NINE

New World Utopias and Dystopias

"The whole world is an America, a new world."
—*Thoreau*[1]

What was new about the "New World"? The "discovery" of America permanently changed the conception of the known world in Europe and beyond. For Amerigo Vespucci, in his 1504 letter called *Mondus Novus*, it was permissible to call the lands a "new World, because nobody before knew of their existence and because it had been commonly believed that the southern hemisphere had been wholly taken up by the ocean."[2] For Francisco López de Gómara, a sixteenth-century chronicler of the Spanish Conquest, "The greatest event since the creation of the world (if we except the incarnation as death of Him who created it) is the discovery of the Indies: that is why they are called the New World."[3] The newly discovered "continent" (soon to become two continents) altered the geographical contours of what until then had been a single hemisphere with three continents—Asia, Africa, and Europe. The maps produced in the century that followed Columbus's voyages bear witness to this.[4]

The physical extension of space was accompanied by the discovery of fauna and flora hitherto unknown and, more tellingly still, of peoples and cultures significantly different from those of the Old World. There is awe and amazement in the observations of some of the conquistadores who accompanied Cortes in his conquest of Mexico: "It is like the enchantments that are told of in the books of Amadís!...And some said: 'are not the things we see a dream?' And he recalled the palaces in which they had been lodged, 'spacious and well built, the walls paneled with cedar and other scented woods,' with great rooms and courts covered with awnings of cotton cloth surrounded by gardens, lily ponds, bathing pools, and sculptured terraces. 'Today,' grieved the veteran conquistador, 'All is overthrown and lost, nothing remains.'"[5] And there were projections onto the newly discovered continent of classical and biblical myths including the Amazons, the Golden Fleece, and the Garden of Eden.[6]

Among other evocations of the New World was the very term Utopia—no place—conceived by Thomas More in his famous essay of that name, published in 1516. The New World would become the repository for transmuted European hopes for an equality and harmony of existence quite unknown in the hierarchically divided and poverty-stricken societies back home: "In America the values and relationships of the Old Continent were inverted: what was bad in the one would be good in the other and vice versa. In this manner, the New World came to be seen as the world of the future, of abundance and fertility; while the Old World was one of the past, of poverty, scarcity and sterility."[7]

It could also become the terrain for new beginnings—political, social, and religious. The Mexican writer, Alfonso Reyes wrote, "After having been foreshadowed by a thousand inklings in mythology and poetry as though it were an inescapable mental concept, America emerged as a geographical reality. And from that moment its role was to enrich the utopian dream of the world, the faith in a better, happier, freer society.... America is essentially a greater possibility for the choice of the good."[8]

The notion of new beginnings was inherent in the religious metaphors of chosen peoples and new Jerusalems discussed in Chapter 2. But it could also take a resolutely secular form. For many the American Revolution, even more than the discovery of the New World, marked a new departure. For instance, Thomas Paine said, "We have it in our power to begin the world over again."[9] Hector St. John de Crèvecoeur, in his *Letters from an American Farmer*, wrote, "Americans are the western pilgrims, who are carrying along with them that great mass of arts, science, vigour, and industry that began long since in the east. They will finish the great circle."[10] And Thomas Jefferson in his First Inaugural Address stated that "Kindly separated by nature and a wide ocean from the exterminating havoc of one quarter of the globe; too high-minded to endure the degradations of the others; possessing a chosen country, with room enough for our descendants to the thousandth and thousandth generation...what more is necessary to make us a happy and a prosperous people?"[11]

The theme of new beginnings continued to haunt the American imagination long afterwards. For Joseph Smith, founder of the Mormons, it was a new world paradise, the cradle of civilization; for Emerson, it inspired and expressed the most expansive and humane spirit; for Melville, Americans bore the ark of the liberties of the world; and Frederick Jackson Turner harnessed it to his reading of the formative role of the frontier in the shaping of the United States.[12]

The American dream continued to fascinate and draw tens of millions of immigrants, who dreamed that its streets were lined with gold; who envisioned the United States as a healing power bringing moral virtue and democratic values to a blood-stained Europe through Woodrow Wilson's 14 Points; and who believed in the four freedoms enumerated by Franklin Delano Roosevelt during World War II and of the new frontier extolled by John F. Kennedy.

Some parts of the continent had even greater claims to embody the American utopian dream, such as California and the western states more generally, with their great canyons, soaring mountains, and Pacific coastline. "Here is the essence of what links America to the world, and a profound source of its global power and influence: the idea that anyone can go to California (or America) and realize their fondest hopes and dreams, because it is open, egalitarian—and rich."[13] For the poet and social critic, William Irving Thompson, "California is not as much a state of the Union as it is an imagi-nation that seceded from our reality a long time ago. In leading the world in the transition from industrial to post-industrial society, California's culture became the first to shift from coal to oil, from steel to plastic, from hardware to software, from reality to fantasy."[14] These were places, even more than the eastern seaboard or south, where the future outweighed the past.

But the United States, as a whole, as the repository of utopian expectations, has always seen itself as a future country. And distinguished outsiders have often shared this creed. The German poet Goethe wrote, "America, you've got it better/Than our old continent. Exult!/You have no decaying castles/And no basalt./Your heart is not troubled,/In lively pursuits,/By useless old remembrance/And empty disputes."[15] And the philosopher Hegel opined, "America is therefore the land of the future, where, in the ages that lie before us, the burden of the World's History shall reveal itself."[16]

Not all have participated in this vision of American destiny. Indigenous Americans were dispossessed of most of their lands and of their way of life. Black Americans were not migrants to the Western Hemisphere of their own free will, and the lot of slaves on the plantations of the American South and elsewhere was anything but utopian. At best, they could dream of freedom from bondage. Even when this came, in the aftermath of the American Civil War and the Emancipation Proclamation, Jim Crow laws followed in their wake. European migrants who came to American shores were also often slow to participate in the Great Barbecue.[17] The bloody suppression of the 1886 Haymarket Riot in Chicago, of the 1894 nationwide Pullman strike, and of miners in the 1921 Battle of Blair Mountain in West Virginia, as well as the endemic slums in major northern cities—all were marks of a country where capital, not labour, reigned supreme in conditions not all that different from the Old World.

There were various attempts to found utopian communities in North America. John and Virginia Friesen have recorded over 100 examples between 1642 and 1900, some religious in inspiration (the Mennonites, the Hutterites, the Doukhobors), others economic (Robert Owen's New Harmony in Indiana and Etienne Cabet's Icaria in Nauvoo, Illinois). "Canada and the United States have a rich history of foresighted men and women who saw what they perceived to be the weaknesses in our social systems... They attempted to build alternative institutions and lifestyles—to develop new ways of looking at society, life, and the universe.... Many immigrants who relocated to North America perceived the opportunity to settle on this continent in utopian terms. They viewed the continent as the land of the second chance."[18] Some of this carried over to the twentieth century in the return to the land movement and the hippie communes of the 1960s, which represented the first fledgling steps of the emerging environmental movement.

When one speaks of utopia, dystopia often lingers in the shadows. Fledgling communal utopias of the nineteenth century fell apart within a generation or two, rent by internal disagreements and by the dominant individualism and capitalism of the larger society. New religions rose and fell with charismatic leaders and often were vulnerable to unfulfilled prophecies of the Second Coming and the like. Or they led to more gruesome outcomes, such as the mass suicides of American followers of preacher Jim Jones in Jonestown, Guyana in 1978 and of members of the Branch Davidian cult during the siege of its headquarters in Waco, Texas in 1993.

Writers captured some of the disenchantment with the American dream. Theodore Dreiser's major work is entitled *An American Tragedy,* while Hart Crane in *The Bridge* notes: "This was the Promised Land, and still it is/

To the persuasive suburban land agent/In bootleg roadhouses where the gin fuzz/Bubbles in time to Hollywood's new love-nest pageant."[19] An uneasy mixture of awe and disillusionment is often mirrored in contemporary American reflections on the country's utopian underpinnings. Writing about the sweeping landscapes celebrated by others, Erica Wagner notes, "Oh sure, there's the desert and there's places like the Grand Canyon, but what do those do to people but make them feel small. You stand at the edge of the Grand Canyon and think, well, just why bother, why bother with anything when there's this thing, millions and millions of years older and bigger than anything I'll ever be? People say it's uplifting, but I think it gets folks down."[20] Lydia Millet records her mixed impressions of Arizona as "a place where the horrible meets the divine" characterized by an "outrageous collision of beauty and tawdriness."[21] And Peggy Orenstein entitles an article on contemporary California, with its budget deficits, foreclosures, and high unemployment, "The Coast of Dystopia."[22]

Factoring in the violence that has never been absent from the American scene, one realizes that the underside of the American dream can be the very opposite of utopian. The list is long and includes not only lynchings but the assassinations of Abraham Lincoln, John F. Kennedy, Bobby Kennedy, and Martin Luther King; school shootings at the University of Texas in 1966, Columbine High School in Colorado in 1999, and Virginia Tech in 2007; and the bombing of the federal office building in Oklahoma City in 1995.

Canada shared some of the same physical grandeur Europeans associated with other parts of the New World. Sir Francis Bond Head, British governor of Upper Canada in the mid-1830s and traveller in South America, observed that "In both the northern and southern hemispheres of the New World, Nature has not only outlined her works on a larger scale, but has painted the whole picture with brighter and more costly colors than she used in delineating and in beautifying the Old World.... The heavens of America appear infinitely higher, the sky is bluer, the air is fresher, the moon looks larger, the stars are brighter, the thunder is louder, the wind is stronger, the rivers longer, the forests bigger, the plains broader."[23]

Canada as "the true north strong and free" has been the stuff of literary and political myth-making from the late nineteenth century on. "We are the Northmen of the New World," wrote Robert Grant Haliburton in 1869. "We are a Northern people—as the true out-crop of human nature, more manly, more real, than the weak, narrow-bones superstition of an effeminate South," wrote William Foster in 1871, in an overtly racist dismissal of the Hispanic portion of the Western Hemisphere.[24] Immigrants were to find here "a promised land," a refuge from Old World travails.[25] Politically, the country was considered to be a Peaceable Kingdom in contrast to lands overseas (or in the Western Hemisphere) where repression and violence often reigned unchecked.

In the same fashion, contemporary exponents of Canadian multiculturalism have been known to extol its virtues in terms bordering on utopian. For Michael Adams, "Canadians are indeed striving toward an increasingly diverse, peaceful, and just society.... In many ways we're on our way to becoming the planet's leading experts in the quiet heroism of getting along."[26] For John Ralston Saul, "The long Canadian experiment with complexity and fairness has never appeared more modern."[27] Whether the Canadian model of multiculturalism is indeed exportable, or could survive the kind of challenges that various European countries have had to face in recent years with the rise of Islamic fundamentalism and increasingly porous boundaries, remains an open question. Multiculturalism is a fair, not a foul weather doctrine.

There is something bleak and potentially frightening lurking in the vast expanses that populate the Canadian mind-set. "The land God gave to Cain," wrote the French explorer, Jacques Cartier, on sighting the coast of Labrador in the sixteenth century.[28] An enduring lesson comes from the mid-nineteenth century fate of the *Franklin*, a British ship frozen in the ice of the Northwest Passage with its 129-man crew; none survived the ordeal. E.J. Pratt described the forging of the Canadian Pacific Railway with shades of horror intersecting with the sheer magnitude of the landscape: "On the North Shore a reptile lay asleep/A hybrid that the myths might have conceived,/But not delivered, as progenitor/Of crawling, gliding things upon the earth./She lay snug in the folds of a huge boa/Whose tail had covered Labrador and swished/Atlantic tides, whose body coiled itself/Around the Hudson Bay, then curled up north/Through Manitoba & Saskatchewan/To Great Slave Lake. In continental reach/The neck went past the Great Bear Lake until/Its head was hidden in the Arctic Seas."[29] No kindly nature here.

As for the human element, Aboriginal people on reserves and off have seen far fewer benefits of the peaceable kingdom than other Canadians. Repression towards other segments of the population has not been lacking in Canadian history, from bloody police and military intervention to end the Winnipeg General Strike in 1919, to the suspension of civil liberties during the October Crisis of 1970, to wholesale police arrests of demonstrators during the G-20 Toronto summit of 2010. Canada has also had its share of home-grown violence, such as the disappearance and murder of over 50 prostitutes from the Downtown Eastside of Vancouver—the world's most livable city until recently according to the *Economist*! Nor has Canada, despite gargantuan efforts, been able to overcome deep national differences in trying to forge a shared sense of national identity. Modesty would better befit Canadians than crowing about Canada as a living paradise on earth.

Mexico has also been called a utopia. Sister Juana Inés de la Cruz, the celebrated Mexican poet of the seventeenth century, described herself as "born/in America, land of plenty,/Gold is my compatriot,/and the precious metals my comrades./Here's a land where sustenance/is almost freely given,/to no other land on earth/is Mother Earth so generous./From the common curse of man/its sons appear to be born free,/for here their daily bread/costs but little sweat of labor."[30] Mexican political figures such as Benito Juárez in the 1850s and José Vasconcelos in the 1920s dreamed of a syncretic fusion of indigenous and European-derived populations, something hammered home in the great mural paintings of Diego Rivera and José Clemente Orozco: "Rivera was possessed with an encyclopedic vision. The totality of *The History of Mexico* [a mural in the Palacio Nacional in Plaza de la Constitucion, Mexico City] is egalitarian, an exhaustive enactment of the artist's faith in the dignity and primacy of the masses."[31] Lomnitz reflected that "Mexican nationalists of the 1920s believed they had caught a glimpse of Utopia in the remnants of the pre-Columbian world as they were refracted in Mexican popular art...pre-Columbian art became Mexico's classical art, its contribution to universal culture."[32] For many fleeing Old World oppression (e.g., Spanish republicans in the aftermath of the Spanish Civil War) or fleeing Latin American dictatorships, Mexico City displayed some of the attributes associated with Paris or London: "Mexico shares with certain cities of America a common characteristic in her hospitality toward free men, many of them exiles—writers, artists, and intellectuals to whom Mexico City has become home."[33]

But Mexico has also written some of the more dystopian pages of North American history. Mexico's indigenous peoples experienced the full brunt of dispossession and extermination in the centuries following the arrival of the conquistadors and continued to do so in modern-day Yucatan, Chiapas, and Oaxaca. Others bore the weight of repressive authority during the Díaz dictatorship, the turmoil of the Mexican Revolution and its aftermath, and more recently in such incidents as the massacre of hundreds of students in Tlatelolco Plaza, Mexico City, on October 2, 1968.

Dystopian refrains echo widely in Mexican political and cultural discourse through the themes of melancholy, inferiority, and solitude found in the works of Mexican writers from Samuel Ramos to Octavio Paz. As the poet José Emilio Pacheco wrote in the aftermath of the Mexico City earthquake of 1985, "Cain our father,/the founder of cities."[34]

The contemporary version of dystopia is the narco-trafficking that is wreaking havoc on the northern and western parts of the country and that has left over 40,000 dead.[35] Ciudad Juárez has a credible claim to be the world's most dangerous city: thousands of its citizens have been murdered or have disappeared, and a three-way war is being waged between two rival drug cartels and the Mexican army.[36] Terms such as "urban Frankenstein" and "pax mafiosa" have been used to describe some of Mexico's northern border cities,[37] which are the scene of earthly apocalypse in Roberto Bolaño's epic novel, 2666. They have also been associated with the black sun of Aztec legend:

> In ancient Mexican lore, there lies behind the sun that shines a black sun that leaves this world to shed light upon another, beneath. The Mexica believed the black sun was carried by the god of the underworld, and was the maleficent herald of death, though not death as finality. The Mexica lived in a condition of expectation of calamity and catastrophe, yet their preoccupation with death was a blend of fear and devotion to the moment of reunion with their ancestors, in the land upon which the black sun shines. And behind the sunlight of the deserts of Amexica—which turns to fire during eventide—there is some maculate, black light that gives nothing back; unshining behind the eternities of space and sky, or the bustle and music in all those labyrinthine streets lined with hot peppers and pistachios tumbling from every open storefront.[38]

Since Mexico was one of the ten leading countries in the world with rates of violent deaths between 1992 and 2002,[39] it is difficult to take seriously Carlos Fuentes's claim that Utopia is both the country's foundation and ultimate destiny.[40] Octavio Paz undoubtedly saw more deeply when he evoked Mexicans' willingness to contemplate horror: "we enjoy our wounds and they enjoy their inventions."[41]

Utopia coexists uneasily with dystopia in New World societies. Still, it is hard to gainsay the hold of utopian expectations for many North Americans at key moments in their histories. The dream of making one's own way in the world, freed from the shackles of the past, played a central part in the exploration and settlement of the continent. And the possibility of starting things afresh, though often debased or thwarted, has been as central to the North American mentality as the hold of the past for many living in Old World societies.

Notes

1 Henry David Thoreau, *Journal, Volume 4: 1851-52*, ed. Leonard N. Neufeldt and Nancy Craig Simmon (Princeton: Princeton University Press, 1992), 421.

2 O'Gorman, *The Invention of America*, 113.

3 Lafaye, *Quetzalcoatl and Guadalupe*, 36.

4 Oswald Dilke and Margaret Dilke, "The Adjustment of Ptolemaic Atlases to Feature the New World," in *The Classical Tradition and the Americas*, Vol. 1 *European Images of the Americas and the Classical Tradition*, ed. Wolfgang Haase and Meyer Reinhold (Berlin/New York: de Gruyter, 1994), 117–34.

5 Bernal Díaz del Castillo, cited in Benjamin Keen, *The Aztec Image in Western Thought* (New Brunswick, NJ: Rutgers University Press, 1971), 14.

6 Jean-Pierre Sanchez, "'El Dorado' and the Myth of the Golden Fleece," in Haase and Reinhold, 339–78.

7 J.L. Abellán, cited in Beatriz Fernández Herrero, *La Utopía de América* (Barcelona: Anthropos, 1992), 93–94; translation by author.

8 Alfonso Reyes, *The Position of America and other Essays* (Freeport: Books for Libraries Press, 1971), 54.

9 Philip Foner, ed., *The Complete Writings of Thomas Paine*, Vol. 1 (New York: The Citadel Press, 1945), 45.

10 M.G.J. de Crèvecoeur, *Letters from an American Farmer* (Philadelphia: Matthew Carey, 1793), Letter III, Para. 55, http://xroads.virginia.edu/~hyper/crev/letter 03.html, accessed December 18, 2011.

11 Thomas Jefferson, First Inaugural Address, March 4, 1801, http://www. bartleby.com/124/pres16.html, accessed December 18, 2011.

12 Turner, "The Frontier in American History"; "European men, institutions, and ideas were lodged in the American wilderness, and the great American West took them to her bosom, taught them a new way of looking on the destiny of the common man, trained them in adaptation to the conditions of the New World, to the creation of new institutions to meet new needs." Cited in Andreas Hess, ed., *American Social and Political Thought: A Concise Introduction* (Edinburgh: Edinburgh University Press, 2000), 23.

13 Cumings, *Dominion from Sea to Sea*, 499.

14 In David Ulin, ed., *Writing Los Angeles: A Literary Anthology* (New York: Library of America, 2002), 631.

15 Goethe, "America, You've Got It Better," http://davidsbuendler.freehostia.com/america.htm, accessed May 20, 2011.

16 Georg Hegel, *Philosophy of History* (New York: Cosimo Classics, 2007), 86.

17 The literary historian, Vernon Parrington, called the period after the American Civil War "the great barbecue": "A huge barbecue was prepared to which all presumably were invited. Not quite all, to be sure; inconspicuous persons, those who were at home, on the farm or at work in the mills and offices were over-looked.... But all the important persons, leading bankers and promoters and businessmen received invitations." Tom Quirk, ed., "Foreword," *The Portable Mark Twain* (New York: Penguin, 2004), xxvii.

18 John W. Friesen and Virginia Lyons Friesen, *The Palgrave Companion to North American Utopias* (London: Macmillan, 2004), 11, 19.

19 Hart Crane, *The Bridge: Quaker Hill*, http://www.poetryfoundation.org/poem/172033, accessed May 20, 2011.

20 Erica Wagner, *Gravity: Stories* (London: Granta, 1997), 204.

21 Lydia Millet, "Arizona," in Matt Weiland and Sean Wilsey, eds., *State by State: A Panoramic Portrait of America* (New York: Harper Collins, 2008), 29.

22 Peggy Orenstein, "The Coast of Dystopia," *New York Times*, January 15, 2010, http://www.nytimes.com/2010/01/17/magazine/17fob-wwln-t.html, accessed December 18, 2011.

23 Cited in Henry David Thoreau, "Walking," in *The American Idea*, ed. Robert Vare (New York: Doubleday, 2007), 437.

24 Berger, *The Sense of Power*, 53, 62–63.

25 Douglas Francis and Chris Kitzan, eds., *The Prairie West as Promised Land* (Calgary: University of Calgary Press), 2007.

26 Michael Adams, *Unlikely Utopia: The Surprising Triumph of Canadian Pluralism* (Toronto: Viking, 2007), 42.

27 John Ralston Saul, *A Fair Country: Telling Truths about Canada* (Toronto: Penguin, 2009), 323.

28 "Land God Gave to Cain," *The Canadian Encyclopedia*, http://www.thecanadianencyclopedia.com/index.cfm?PgNm=TCE&Params=A1ARTA0004499, accessed December 18, 2011.

29 E.J. Pratt, "Towards the Last Spike," in *Selected Poems* (Toronto: University of Toronto Press, 2000), 181–82.

30 Juana Inés de la Cruz, cited in Lafaye, *Quetzalcoatl and Guadalupe*, 71.

31 Baldwin, *The Plumed Serpent*, 150.

32 Claudio Lomnitz, "Final Reflections: What Was Mexico's Cultural Revolution?" in *The Eagle and the Virgin: National Identity, Utopia and Memory in*

Mexico, 1920–1940, ed. Mary Kay Vaughan (Durham: Duke University Press, 2006), 342, 347.

33 Arciniegas, *Latin America*, 501; In the same vein, Enrique Krauze writes: "Cárdenas's Mexico became—and Mexico continues to be—a country of asylum for the persecuted of other lands." *Mexico: Biography of Power*, 476.

34 Pacheco, *City of Memory*, 185.

35 BBC, "Q&A: Mexico's Drug-related Violence," August 26, 2011, http://www.bbc.co.uk/news/world-latin-america-10681249, accessed December 18, 2011.

36 Jeremy Fox, "Mexnarcos," *Open Democracy*, January 17, 2011, http://www.opendemocracy.net/jeremy-fox/mexnarcos, accessed December 18, 2011.

37 Ed Vulliamy, *Amexica: War along the Borderlines* (New York: Farrar, Straus and Giroux, 2010), chaps. 4, 8.

38 Vulliamy, *Amexica*, 321.

39 Abel Perez Zamorano, "Los problemas estructurales del campo mexicano," in *México, Visión Global*, ed. Miguel Godínez and Alberto Martínez (Mexico: Porrua, 2006), 209.

40 Carlos Fuentes, "We Were Founded as Utopia; Utopia Is Our Destiny," in his *The Buried Mirror: Reflections on Spain and the New World* (Boston: Houghton Miflin Harcourt, 1999), 126.

41 Paz, *Labyrinth of Solitude*, 24, 25.

TEN

An Archipelago of Regions

"I am larger...I contain multitudes"
—Walt Whitman, Song of Myself [1]

Formally, North America consists of three countries, each with its own national characteristics and identity. In fact, each of these countries consists of discrete regional entities, with a number of cross-border regions to boot.

Since all three countries are federal states, it would seem fairly easy to delineate these. Canada has ten provinces and three territories; the United States has 50 states and one federal district; Mexico has 31 states and one federal district. This makes 96 units in all. Residents may have strong provincial or state loyalties that, at times, have been known to trump national ones.

The concept of region, however, is not one and the same with that of province or state. There are regions within provinces and states—rural vs. urban, eastern vs. western, water-rich vs. water-poor—that may undercut any strictly state-wide or province-wide identity. There are larger geographical groupings that constitute their own regional units, such as the Maritime provinces, the Prairies, and the North within Canada; New England, the mid-Atlantic, the South, the Midwest, the Rocky Mountain states, and the Pacific Northwest in the United States; and the border states of northern Mexico, central Mexico, Yucatan, and the southern states bordering Central America. As Louis Mumford once noted, "Between the continent and the historic village is an area sometimes larger, sometimes smaller than a political state. It is a human region."[2]

Geography is only one dimension of regional distinctiveness. Economic underpinnings are another, from agricultural to financial, industrial, resource-base, or high tech. The same is true where religious identification, ethnic and linguistic characteristics, and political orientation are concerned. North America is a continent with multiple regional identities, overlapping the national boundaries that compose it.

Fischer has described the four strains of liberty that composed the original 13 Colonies as follows: ordered—Puritan and New England; hierarchical—Cavalier and Coastal South; reciprocal—Quaker and mid-Atlantic; natural—backcountry and Southwest interior.[3] Each has left its mark on American development, speech patterns, and underlying values. The division between free and slave states dominated politics until the Civil War. However, that war did not put an end to a distinct sense of Southern identity. As Charles Reagan Wilson describes it, "The dream of a separate southern identity did not die in 1865. A Southern political nation was not to be...but the dream of a cohesive Southern people with a separate cultural identity replaced the original longing."[4] Or as William Faulkner put it even more tellingly in *Requiem for a Nun,* "The past is never dead. It's not even past."[5]

Despite the 13 Colonies' British roots on the Atlantic seaboard, westward expansion and the opening of the country to settlement by Europeans and others put a very different stamp on American national identity, famously illustrated in Frederick Jackson Turner's 1891 thesis about the role of the frontier in American history. For his part, Bruce Cumings has extended the analysis to the Pacific, discussing the impact of World War II in particular, in completing the extension of a national market across the continent.[6]

A sense of state and regional identity runs deep in the United States. The inhabitants of Massachusetts and New England more generally are conscious of the historical importance of their region in the formation of the country. "For a long time, New England was *the* quintessential American region.... New England was the birthplace not only of the small town, but also, arguably, of the industrial city.... New England in a broader sense [became] inextricably linked to the national culture.... New England writers [such as Emerson, Thoreau, Hawthorne, Melville, and Dickinson] have defined the national cultural tradition."[7] New York likes to think of itself as the Empire State, and New York City has been the financial, media, and cultural centre of the United States (to the chagrin of many living in the other regions of the country). The Midwest was long associated with an agrarian-republican spirit of independence, populist democracy, and values of honour and neighbourly mutuality.[8] The American West is the region most associated with the myths, justifications, and rationales of American expansion and conquest.[9] Its rising importance coincides with the displacement of economic power from the Atlantic to the Pacific that is currently underway. The Pacific Southwest is simultaneously the region most closely tied to Mexico, with large Latino populations and closely connected cross-border cities.

Regions, however, are not political actors—states are. States can have their own specific identities, nicely illustrated in a recent collection by 50 different American writers.[10] The states, to invoke a phrase usually attributed to Justice Louis Brandeis, can act "as laboratories of democracy."[11] They can experiment with devices such as initiative and recall, with legislation on capital punishment or civil marriage, with environmental legislation or welfare reform. States can also prove to be what I would call "laboratories of reaction," as underlined by segregation in various southern states for over a century, current attempts to limit illegal immigration in Arizona, and anti-labour offensives in Wisconsin and elsewhere. Moreover, obstreperous state governors such as Huey Long of Louisiana and George Wallace of Alabama have come close to exercising despotic rule within their own fiefdoms. Federalism can prove to be both a many splendoured and a bluntly tempered device.

In the Canadian case, as we have seen throughout this book, English-French duality has been a key element of Canadian federalism from the beginning. For all the "Britishness" of the inhabitants of Atlantic Canada or Upper Canada/Ontario, the presence of a French-speaking majority in Quebec made impossible the kind of ethnic or linguistic unity to which Anglophones aspired.

Canada is a federal state with formal equality among its ten provinces. In important respects, however, it is a multinational federation where Quebec and Aboriginal peoples are concerned. Quebec has achieved a form of special status within Confederation, not through mega-constitutional changes, but through a series of one-on-one arrangements that have helped to keep the federation afloat. Special status, symbolically or in practice, may well be the pragmatic Canadian way of dealing with specific Quebec demands. At the same time, Canada is a country of regions, as Northrop Frye noted,[12] or of "limited identities" to evoke a term first advanced by the historian Maurice Careless.[13]

Ontario, as the commercial, financial, and manufacturing centre of the country, with some 40 per cent of Canada's population, has not been inclined to think of itself as a region apart—at least not until recently. It tended to identify itself with Canada as a whole, all the more easily since its influence over federal governments, whatever their stripe, has been larger than most. It is only in recent decades that Ontario's relative economic performance has become a cause of concern. In a sense, Ontario has to cease being a region that dares not speak its name. Its role, within the larger Canadian ensemble, is that of the heartland of the country.

Atlantic Canada is the least populous of southern Canada's regions. It has also tended to be the poorest, significantly more reliant on equalization payments than the others. Does regional identity trump provincial identities? Not very much, judging by the failure of repeated attempts to float the idea of Maritime union and by Newfoundland's clear sense of being a province unto itself.

For some the West is a single region of Canada. For example, the Canada West Foundation has published oodles of material extolling the West's place within Confederation and defending its regional interests. Significantly, the Foundation is headquartered in Calgary—not Vancouver—and its vision of a single West does not really jibe with views on the other side of the Rockies. The best modern book on British Columbia history is called *The West beyond the West*.[14] In a number of respects the province's differences with Prairie Canada are striking. British Columbia has had a much more turbulent history of class conflict and political polarization than Alberta, which has been a one-party province most of the time, and a conservative one at that. British Columbia has a much stronger environmental movement, tending to align itself closely on the climate initiatives of a state such as California. It is an increasingly multicultural province, despite an earlier history of racism and exclusion toward Asians. It has the highest percentage of Canadians by far—35 per cent—who profess no belief in God. And it sees its vocation as lying on the shores of the Pacific, the cutting edge of global economic activity in the twenty-first century.

Prairie Canada is another matter, and here Alberta, flush with its wealth from oil and natural gas, is clearly the ascendant province. More than that, Alberta politicians have been better at playing the national political game—or more willing to do so—than their Pacific counterparts. Strongly conservative parties such as Reform and the Canadian Alliance were born in Alberta. Albertans Joe Clark, Preston Manning, and Stephen Harper have made their mark federally. But within Prairie Canada, provincial loyalties remain strong. Manitoba and Saskatchewan have their own political traditions and cultures, while Albertans are the ones who preen themselves on the so-called Alberta advantage—the lowest personal taxes in Canada, the only province without a sales tax, and a province with a hefty Heritage Fund (albeit a mere shadow of what Norway, another oil rich jurisdiction, has been able to put aside). Alberta is also Canada's "red" province in the American sense of red and blue states. Its residents tend to be more conservative in their leanings than most, more given to believe in the virtues of a relatively unregulated market capitalism, and more critical of controls on individual liberty such as carrying a gun.

What of the North? This is a huge land mass with a very thin population, major differences between Aboriginal and non-Aboriginal residents, and territories with something of a trustee relationship with the federal government. The North also finds itself at the centre of one of the unfolding dramas of the twenty-first century—climate change—with the High Arctic experiencing serious melting of the icecaps and warming of the seas. The potential opening of the Arctic to ocean navigation—the Northwest Passage revisited—may also spark significant disputes over sovereignty in the High Arctic and concerns about potential environmental damage.

A quite different way of thinking about region is in terms of cross-border entities. For certain purposes, these do matter. Ontario and the Midwest American states cooperate over water resources in the Great Lakes; Quebec and Atlantic premiers and their New England state counterparts periodically meet; the links between British Columbia and the Northwest Pacific states are sufficiently close that the region is sometimes referred to as Cascadia; and California and Mexico's Baja California and Texas and the northeast Mexican states of Chihuahua, Coahuila, Nuevo Laredo, and Tamaulipas are both closely tied. None of these groupings is about to displace the larger nation-states to which the different units belong, but they underline the point that population flows, resources, trade, manufacturing, and environmental issues cross national boundaries and have their own ways of forging cross-border ties. As the historian Sam Truett argues, "Borderlands history provides a space for 'decentering' national and imperial narratives.... It offers a framework for thinking about US history *and* Mexican history...about the American *and* Canadian Wests."[15] As Victor Konrad and Heather Nichol state, "[T]he borderland is a zone of interaction where people on one side of the border share values, beliefs, feelings, and expectations with people on the other side of the border.... [B]orderlands may be seen on a continuum from border regions with little evidence of integration to fully developed, interactive zones which show substantive linkage in trade, cross-border policy integration, institutional alignment and cultural belonging."[16] In a more critical vein, however, Fernando Romero notes, "many would claim that the overall effects of [NAFTA] on Mexico, the US, and the border region have been largely detrimental and have not brought widespread prosperity and development."[17]

Mexico, despite a common experience of Spanish rule for three centuries, contains within its borders four or five distinct societies. In the words of Carlos Fuentes, "It's a thousand countries with a single name.... You will bring with you the red deserts, the steppes of prickly pears and maguey, the world of the nopal, the belt of lava and frozen craters, the walls with golden church cupolas and stone battlements, the cities of red *tezontle*, the towns of adobe, the paths of black mud...the fine bones of Michoacán, the diminutive flesh of Tlaxcala, the Miztec tresses, Puebla marquetry, Jalisco glass, Oaxaca jade...they've gotten into your gut."[18] In a less poetic vein are the very different patterns of development Mexico's regions have experienced.

The northern tier of states, with their desert-like climate, were little touched by the Meso-American civilizations of central and southern Mexico. Given their proximity to the United States, they have been more subject to American influence from the nineteenth century on. They developed more diversified economies than the single-crop plantation economies to the south[19] and played a key role in the Mexican Revolution, contributing some of its leading generals and political figures. They remain among Mexico's most prosperous states to this day. As Sidney Weintraub notes, "[Mexico's] border region's gross GDP grew by 57% from 1993 (the year before NAFTA came into effect) to 2004, compared to GDP growth of 30% for the rest of the country. From 2000 to 2005, Mexico's population grew by 1.1%, while that of Baja California North grew by 2.7%, Tamaulipas by almost 2%, and Nuevo Léon by almost 1.7%."[20] At the same time, as Iguiniz and Labazee observe, "The problem of the region's [the north's] cultural absorption by the US remains acute. Its population lacks a distinct personality, since migrants have come from all over the country.... English is widely spoken, with English signs to be seen everywhere and anglicisms creeping into local Spanish. A majority of *fronterizos* work for American companies or families, consume American products, and watch American television programs."[21]

The semi-arid mountainous states—Hidalgo, Tlaxcala, Puebla, Morelos, Guerrero, México, and Querétaro—comprise a distinct *mestizo* region.[22] With their old grain-producing haciendas and Spanish-derived architecture, they constitute the heartland of the country and the backbone of its democratization and political reform.[23]

Mexico City—*el monstruo,* as it is sometimes called—is the world's single largest metropolis and encompasses 20 million inhabitants in its extended conurbation. It embodies the same concentration of political, economic, and cultural power one associates with world capital cities such as London, Paris, Moscow, and Tokyo, but it has problems of sustainability and liveability that eclipse the others.[24] Although for long the seat of concentrated governmental power and authoritarianism, it has also served as the centre of major critical thought, spawning social actors with strong ties to the opposition.[25]

The southern states of Chiapas, Oaxaca, and Guerrero are the poorest in the country when measured by criteria such as GDP per capita;[26] not coincidentally, they also contain the largest indigenous populations as well. The Yucatan Peninsula, the site of vanished Mayan civilization, was for long an area of indentured labour. In recent decades, it has become a major centre of Mexican tourism, with complexes such as Cancún and Playa del Carmen catering to international arrivals.[27] Its three states—Quintana Roo, Yucatan, and Campeche—not unlike Prairie Canada's three provinces, have developed distinctive political traditions of their own.[28]

Two characteristics of Mexican federalism are worth noting. For long it was characterized by a strongly centralized structure that made many state governors during the long PRI reign de facto viceroys within a clientilist political system.[29] At the same time, those governors could become *caciques,* strong autocratic rulers in local and regional affairs. A recent example is Ulises Ruíz Ortiz in Oaxaca, whose use of paramilitary forces against striking teachers and an opposition radio station in 2006 provoked widespread concerns about civil liberties at the state level.[30] However, the emergence of greater democratic pluralism in Mexico has also made federalism a more authentic expression of regional political sentiments than before.[31] In the words of a former Speaker of the Mexican Senate, "Representative democracy, political pluralism, social diversity oblige us to avoid simulation, to stop disguising centralism, and to promote the value of federal unity."[32]

Regions constitute important building blocks of the North American continent. They play a formative role in shaping identities. Cormac McCarthy, in describing the cowboys of Texas and of northern Mexico, writes, "They [the *vaqueros,* cowboys] said that the weather and seasons that form a land mass form also the inner fortunes of men in their generations and are passed on to their children and are not so easily come by otherwise."[33] Writing about the Pacific Northwest, Douglas Todd states that "Idealism has become a way of life for many, a kind of shared civil, or secular religion—based on reverence for nature and hope for the future."[34] One can say of North America's regions what the Czech writer, Karl Čapek, said of Europe's nation-states: "The creator of Europe made her small and even split her up into little parts, so that our hearts could find joy not in size but in plurality."[35]

Notes

1 Walt Whitman, "Song of Myself," #51, in Whitman, *Complete Poetry and Collected Prose*, 246.

2 Louis Mumford, cited in Howard Odum and Henry Moore, eds., *American Regionalism: A Cultural Historical Approach to National Integration* (New York: Henry Holt, 1938), 2.

3 Fischer, *Albion's Seed*, 897–98.

4 Charles Reagan Wilson, *Baptised in Blood: The Religion of the Lost Cause, 1865–1920* (Athens: University of Georgia Press, 2009), 1.

5 William Faulkner, "Gavin Stevens, Act 1, Scene III," *Requiem for a Nun* (New York: Random House, 1951).

6 Cumings, *Dominion from Sea to Sea*, 333.

7 Stephen Nissenbaum, "Inventing New England," in *The New Regionalism*, ed. Charles Reagan Wilson (Jackson: University Press of Mississippi, 1998), 105–07.

8 Walter Prescott Webb, *The Great Plains*, cited in Robert L. Dorman, "The Regionalist Movement in America," in Wilson, *The New Regionalism*, 9.

9 Patricia Nelson Limerick, "The Realization of the American West," in Wilson, *The New Regionalism*, 73–75.

10 See Weiland and Wilsey, *State by State*.

11 Justice Louis Brandeis, dissenting opinion, United States Supreme Court, *New State Ice Co. vs. Liebmann*, 285 US 262 (1932). Brandeis actually wrote: "It is one of the happy merits of the federal system that a single courageous state may, if its citizens choose, serve as a laboratory; and try novel social and economic experiments." This has been cited frequently as though Brandeis had described the states as "laboratories of democracy."

12 "The question of Canadian identity, so far as it affects the creative imagination, is not a 'Canadian' question at all, but a regional question." Northrop Frye, *The Bush Garden: Essays on the Canadian Imagination* (Toronto: Anansi, 1971), xxii.

13 Maurice Careless, "Limited Identities in Canada," *Canadian Historical Review* 50 (1969): 1–10.

14 Jean Barman, *The West beyond the West: A History of British Columbia*, 3rd ed. (Toronto: University of Toronto Press, 2007).

15 Cited in Sterling Evans, ed., "Afterward," *The Borderlands of the Canadian and American Wests* (Lincoln: University of Nebraska Press, 2006), 359.

16 Victor Konrad and Heather Nicol, *Beyond Walls: Re-inventing the Canada-United States Borderlands* (Aldershot: Ashgate, 2008), 2–3.

17 Fernando Romero, *Hyper-Border: The Contemporary US-Mexico Border and Its Future* (New York: Princeton Architectural Press, 2008), 42.

18 Carlos Fuentes, "Artemio Cruz," cited in von Delden, *Carlos Fuentes, Mexico, and Modernity*, 149.

19 Robert Buffington and William French, "The Culture of Modernity," in *The Oxford History of Mexico*, ed. Michael Meyer and William Beezley (New York: Oxford University Press, 2000), 401.

20 Weintraub, *Unequal Partners*, 117.

21 Margarita Estrada Iguiniz and Pascal Labazee, eds., *Globalización y localidad: espacios, actores, movilidades e identidades* (Mexico: Ciesas, 2007), 300.

22 Victoria Rodriguez, *Decentralization in Mexico: From Reforma Municipal to Solidaridad to Nuevo Federalismo* (Boulder: Westview, 1997), 289.

23 Vincente Fox, August 6, 1998, cited in Shorris, *The Life and Times of Mexico*, 461.

24 "[T]he giant amoeba of Mexico City is extending pseudopods that will eventually incorporate much of central Mexico into a single megalopolis with a mid-21st century population of approximately 50 million—about 40% of the national total." Mike Davis, *Planet of Slums* (London: Verso, 2006), 5.

25 Silvia Gomez Tagle, "Nuevas Formaciones Políticas en el Distrito Federal," in *La Geografía del Poder y las Elecciones in México*, ed. Silvia Gomez Tagle and Maria Eugenia Valdes (Mexico: Plaza y Valdes, 2000), 41.

26 Velasco, *Insurgency, Authoritarianism*, 34–35.

27 Ronald Mize and Alicia Swords, *Consuming Mexican Labor: From the Bracero Program to NAFTA* (Toronto: University of Toronto Press, 2011), 206–08.

28 Tagle, "Nuevas Formaciones Políticas en el Distrito Federal," 17.

29 Acosta Romero, "Mexican federalism is an aspiration punctuated by the reality of an undeniable centralism [and] an increasingly pervasive presidency." Cited in Rodriguez, *Decentralization in Mexico*, 17.

30 John Gibler, "Teacher Rebellion in Oaxaca," *In These Times*, August 21, 2006, http://www.inthesetimes.com/article/2795/, accessed December 20, 2011.

31 Cf. Tonatiuh Guillén López, "Federalism and the Reform of Political Power," in *Mexico's Democratic Challenges*, ed. Andrew Selee and Jacqueline Peschard (Washington: Woodrow Wilson Center Press, 2010), 187–202.

32 Senator Enrique Jackson Ramírez, "Presentación," in *Federalismo y relaciones intergubernamentales*, ed. Mariano Palacios Alcocer (Mexico: Senado de la República, 2003), 7.

33 Cormac McCarthy, *All the Pretty Horses* (New York: Knopf, 1992), 226.

34 Douglas Todd, ed., *Cascadia: The Elusive Utopia* (Vancouver: Ronsdale Press, 2008), 18.

35 Karl Čapek, cited in Tony Judt, *Postwar: A History of Europe Since 1945* (New York: Penguin, 2005), 749.

ELEVEN

A North American Civilization?

"From the European world are no precedents to be drawn for a people who
think they are capable of governing themselves."
—*Charles Pinckney, South Carolina politician,*
signer of the American Constitution[1]

To what degree can one speak of North America constituting a new civilization? Charles and Mary Beard used the term in their 1927 history of the United States, so describing its politics, economics, technology, philosophy, science, religion, education, and literature.[2] Harold Laski talked about Americanism as a principle of civilization, emphasizing the restlessness and non-conformism that characterized the country and the unmistakably New World character of American culture.[3] Max Lerner argued that America was not a European civilization and that it, not Europe, had become the centre of Western power.[4] American influence at the global level has been paramount since 1945. Even more so, the United States has been the central actor in the moulding of what one might call a North American way of life or civilization.

The inhabitants of the United States, far more than those of neighbouring North American societies to its north or south, were conscious of its newness, of its future orientation, of their striking out on their own. As Louis Hartz stated, "The New World did not merely offer the Americans a virgin ground for the building of a liberal system; it conspired itself to help that system along. The abundance of land in America, as well as the need to lure new settlers, entered it completely at every point.... The point of departure of great revolutionary thought everywhere else in the world has been the effort to build a new society on the ruins of an old one, and this is an experience America has never had. We are reminded again of Tocqueville's statement that Americans are 'born equal.'"[5] Theodore H. White added, "Americans are not a people like the French, Germans, or Japanese, whose genes have been mixing with kindred genes for thousands of years. Americans are held together only by ideas."[6]

One of those ideas was pragmatism, as American a philosophy as any. In the words of William James, "A pragmatist turns his back resolutely and once and for all upon a lot of inveterate habits dear to professional philosophers. He turns away from verbal solutions, from bad a priori principles, closed systems, and pretended absolutes and origins. He turns towards concreteness and adequacy, towards facts, towards action, and towards power."[7] The emphasis of its proponents was on future-orientation, contingency, and the benefits of thinking through experience over abstract rationalism.

What was missing in the American situation was a sense of the tragic. Although as individuals Americans might well experience anxiety and despair, the country as a whole, with the possible exception of the Civil War period, has largely avoided "the missed opportunities, fatal choices, conclusive and irrevocable defeats"[8] experienced by so many other societies. In place of the tragic, the American temperament has been one of sunny optimism and bold initiatives. As Albert Einstein once wrote of Americans, they were a people "always coming, never being."[9]

Perhaps the most fitting metaphor for interpreting the United States was coined by Thomas Mann. Forced into exile in California during the Third Reich, he had reason enough to contemplate the differences between Europe and the United States. It led him to observe that "The future belongs to the man of today, whose mind and 'common sense' are directed toward the nearest, most useful matters; it belongs to him whose energy is not tainted by the pallor of thought. Not only Germany, all of Europe is Hamlet, and Fortinbras is America."[10]

There is plenty in the American experience to back up this emphasis on action over contemplation: the harnessing of technology and science to innovation; experimentation with democratic principles at various levels of government; a new type of urban architecture, with the skyscraper as its icon; the automobile, with the highways, suburbia, exurbia, and expanded carbon footprints that have accompanied it; mass public consumption; Hollywood and Madison Avenue; jazz and rock'n'roll; TV game shows; the Internet and Facebook. The list could go on and on.

The upshot is an American civilization quite distinctive and dynamic in its characteristics. One key feature is the contrast between a young dynamic society, adventurous in spirit and impatient with constraint, and the tired Old World from which much of its population had come.[11] Another is the orientation to the future in contrast with that of societies where the stranglehold of the past is omnipresent. Yet a third is the notion of establishing a new order for the ages, a *novus ordo seclorum*, to cite the Great Seal of 1782, with such underlying features as individual liberty, political equality, religious freedom, and economic enterprise.[12]

If there is a distinctly North American civilization, one thinks of it as American civilization. More than any other New World society, the United States has risen to the challenge of "establishing new societies which were, and yet were not, replicas of the ones which the settlers had left behind in Europe; the challenge of establishing a distinctive sense of identity and of cutting the umbilical cords that bound them to their mother countries."[13] One speaks of an American creed, not of a Canadian or Mexican one. The very name, the United States of America, has come to be associated with the noun "America" as is true for the adjective "American" in many languages, to the chagrin, no doubt, of the hundreds of millions of inhabitants of the Americas who do not live in the United States. It is American historians, not Canadian or Mexican, who celebrate their history in terms of a magic transformation or evoke a series of domains where the United States has come to symbolize civilizational innovation.[14] It is American hard power and soft power that constitute the subject of both attraction and repulsion around the world. Admirers of American civilization have had recourse to terms such as Columbia, God's country, or land of liberty in describing the United States. Its critics, especially numerous in Latin America, have invoked terms such as Caliban, Colossus of the North, the Monster, or Nimrod. But if we embrace a more even-tempered metaphor such as Thomas Mann's Fortinbras to symbolize the United States, where does this leave Canada and Mexico by comparison?

Canadians, to invoke Harold Innis, the economic historian, have inhabited a hard frontier, rather than a soft one.[15] Their history has been one of adapting to geography, harnessing technology, and expanding westward. To this degree they share the Fortinbras qualities associated with the United States. But the Canadian Shield constituted a major obstacle to settlement, and the vast northern territories of Canada a very different terrain from the more temperate country to the south. The latter has given rise to occasional northern visions, such as that of John Diefenbaker back in the

1950s, and to musings about *nordicity* by writers and social scientists.[16] But this is small potatoes compared to a much more widespread characteristic of the Canadian mind-set, associated with living in a vast, harsh, and thinly populated territory—self-doubt.

Countries with small populations often have an inferiority complex toward larger, more powerful neighbours. And when that neighbour is a global power like the United States, with manifest destiny in its mind-set, it makes it difficult for the smaller country to avoid the negative comparisons that can follow. Canada has been less dynamic than the United States economically and technologically. Its standard of living, while high, has never been quite as high, nor has its productivity been able to keep pace. Demographically, a larger number of Canadians have migrated to the United States since the nineteenth century than Americans to Canada. Politically, dramatic events have not been Canada's forte, which is a polite way of saying that a long-prevalent colonial mentality and pattern of slow evolutionary change make for a dull, plodding historical narrative when compared to its neighbour. It also reinforces a negative characteristic of the Canadian national temperament—an emphasis on not being American is a core feature of Canadian identity.

Survivalism as national ideology makes for thin gruel. It plays into a Hamlet-like disposition, a continuous and renewed preoccupation with the United States as a symbolic foil for deeper anxieties. Canadian elections—for instance, in 1891, 1911, 1963, and 1988—have been fought over Canadian-American relations, even while dirges and lamentations about the country surviving an inevitable American takeover have been something of a Canadian academic and literary obsession. This makes it impossible to think of Canada as representing something civilizationally unique, in the way that has often characterized visions of the United States. If anything, Canada becomes a participant in a common North American civilization, although a slightly more tepid version of the American, with vestiges of British and, to a lesser degree, French influences. This is not entirely fair to a country that in the social arena has proven significantly more egalitarian than the United States, in the cultural and intellectual domains one that increasingly punches above its weight, and in its foreign policy one—until Stephen Harper came along—with a more characteristically multilateral outlook than its neighbour to the south. *Mais c'est la vie*—as they say in Canada's other official language.

Evoking that other language underlines another aspect of Canada's Hamlet-like disposition, that is, its preoccupation with survival as a multinational federation. Ever since its foundation—indeed, even before—Canada has had to deal with the reality of two major linguistic groups dwelling side by side. Quebec, the principal home base of Canada's francophones, began its existence as New France and only fell under British rule as a result of the Seven Years' War. While able to preserve both language and religion as inhabitants of a British colony, some French Canadians dreamed of independence, only to see those dreams crushed in the aftermath of the rebellions of 1837–38. Quebec and its French-Canadian majority acquired significant autonomy with Canadian Confederation. A concern for survival, as the sole majority French-speaking society in North America, has been a constant theme throughout its subsequent history. This has resulted in a feeling that Quebec's sensibilities as the homeland of a minority nationality are not always understood or respected by English Canadians. It has led to battles over the place of French, and of the English-speaking minority, within Quebec. It has fuelled the sovereignty movement, which came into its own after 1960. And it has engendered a deep melancholy within the Quebec mind-frame,[17] the fate of being a minority nationality within a larger territorial ensemble.

English Canada has had its own reasons to be unhappy with French Canada. During the two world wars, French Canadians opposed conscription in large numbers when their English-Canadian counterparts rallied to the flag. Quebec has often opposed what it sees as centralizing initiatives by the federal government, a government that most English Canadians accept as their national government. And twice in the postwar period, in 1980 and 1995, Quebec held a referendum on potential separation from Canada, with the outcome on the second occasion a razor-thin victory for the federalist side. Whatever else Canada may be, it has not forged the kind of national unity—*e pluribus unum*—that Americans (admittedly after a bloody civil war) have attained. This leaves a perpetually unresolved and unresolvable conundrum, where neither side fully understands the other's point of view and where the possibility of breakup lurks in the background. "To be or not to be" is the recurring Canadian national question.

This makes it difficult to make hubristic claims of the type Americans put forward. Not that Canadians haven't tried. Some have invoked Canada's relative success in binational coexistence as a model for others, though arguably Switzerland has done at least as well as Canada at reconciling different linguistic groups. Others hark on Canadian multiculturalism as a model for the world, though there have been fewer and fewer takers, as one European country after another has turned its back on the very concept.

The occasional outsider, such as the historian Felipe Fernández-Armesto, may point to Canada as a model New World society:

> Despite a paucity of population, Canada has become home to one of the world's biggest economies. ... In the twentieth century Canada developed a reputation second to none in the hallmark virtues of a civil society: adherence to democracy, respect for human rights, accommodation of ethnic minorities, values of pluralism and multiculturalism, generous and efficient promotion of social welfare, and commitment of the pursuit of peace. ... Its political stability has exceeded even that of the United States. ... Canada is close to being most people's ideal country.[18]

This is very flattering to Canadian ears, no doubt. But it is not the Canadian tail that wags the North American dog. Not by a long-shot. Nor does it make it any more plausible to think of Canada as constituting a civilization unto itself. Long beholden to metropolitan European powers, culturally, economically, and politically, subsequently no less beholden to the United States, Canada remains at best the Scandinavia of North America, not its continental heartland.

Where does Mexico fit into the North American civilizational ensemble? Mexico is a combination of at least three elements. One is a privileging of time over space, with the archaeological past a living part of Mexican identity. A second is a Mexican version of the Hamlet theme, with a darker, more tragic underpinning to it than in the Canadian case. And the third is a variant of what Albert Camus referred to as *la pensée de midi,* a southern mentality or way of thinking, different from the more materially driven mentality of the two countries to its north.

The pre-Columbian past infuses Mexican identity. Roger Batra speaks of "the modern myth of the stooping hero, hallowed by Diego Rivera as the man in his *sarape*... [of] wounded aboriginal virtues never to be seen again."[19] The editors of an anthology of Mexican poetry describe Mexico as "not merely a cheap place for poets to live in magnificent scenery... it was, unlike the United States, a place where the history of the Americas, and the cycles of history itself, were visible on every corner."[20] No less tellingly, President López Mateos, who commissioned the National Museum of Anthropology in Mexico City with its vast collection of pre-Columbian artifacts, told the architect who directed its construction, "On leaving the museum, the Mexican [should] feel proud to be Mexican."[21] This monumentalization of the Mexican past does not, however, undo the deep divide between indigenous and non-indigenous peoples in Mexican society. Earl Shorris writes about the "unresolved conflict between two faces of Mexico, [the] poor indigenous and [the] rich and middle-class European side...the rich side in the soul of every Mexican despises the darkness of the poor, so the poor side in return despises the whiteness of the rich."[22] All this underlines a tragic dimension in the Mexican predicament that other elements reinforce.

A striking feature of Mexican popular culture is the veneration of the dead. *El dia de los muertos* (the Day of the Dead)—overlapping November 1 and 2—is a major holiday, with visits to the cemetery, food offerings to the dead, and the omnipresence of *calaveras,* candy skulls. The skeletal images of engraver José Guadalupe Posada made their entry into the high art of the twentieth century, appearing in some of Diego Rivera's and Frida Kahlo's paintings, as well as into the cartoon culture of the country. The anthropologist Claudio Lomnitz invokes death as Mexico's national totem.[23] If he is right, it could be argued that Mexico embodies the *memento mori* theme—"remember your mortality"—embedded in European medieval and early modern culture, something that can be contrasted with the American emphasis on the pursuit of happiness. Life is not always about achieving happiness or having a good day. It is also about facing mortality.

A parallel trait that a number of commentators have associated with Mexico is melancholy—Hamlet's trait par excellence. As Batra observes "Since the nineteenth century, the Mexican intelligentsia...has believed that only melancholic rapture could facilitate communication between Mexicans and the ancient profound strata of a native land that has been built outside history, at the wrong moment and with the use of scrap materials. For this reason, so many Mexican intellectuals have chosen to use the ink of melancholy in their depictions of the national culture."[24] Alfonso Reyes, one of Mexico's more celebrated twentieth-century essayists, lamented, "We were invited to the banquet of civilization after the meal had already been served."[25] Octavio Paz contrasted the United States with his country, saying that "The United States is a society that wants to realize its ideals, has no wish to exchange them for others, and is confident of surviving...the Mexican's characteristic is his willingness to contemplate horror...They [Americans] are optimists and we are nihilists."[26] And Lomnitz notes that Mexico's national heroes were the martyred and defeated Cuauhtémoc and Pancho Villa rather than a triumphant Símon Bolívar.[27]

This sense of inadequacy or failure, of what in Quebec was historically described as *être né pour un petit pain*—being born for small things—would be overwhelming were it not compensated by another feature of

Mexican identity, a folkloric wisdom grounded in the sounds and colours and smells of a country of the south. Physical setting is part of the story—the warmth and light that attract snowbirds by the millions from both the United States and Canada every year. But it goes beyond climate and influences mentality, much as Montesquieu might have argued in *The Spirit of the Laws*. A passage from Daniel Cosío Villegas, one of Mexico's most esteemed twentieth-century academics, speaks to this point:

> The Mexican did not seek wealth as eagerly as he sought the liberty and the necessary calm to find his chosen way, the physical leisure to pursue it, and the solitude to enjoy it.... A sensitive man in spite of his chapped feet, cracked open from so much walking barefoot over rocks and mire, the Mexican possesses an artistic feeling and capacity.... He rejoices before a landscape, he is entranced in studying a human face or contemplating a religious image; colors move him.... The world in which he has lived has not been a material world, but more, much more, a spiritual and religious one.[28]

A more metaphysical outlook on life, when compared to the instrumental civilization to the north, is closer to the world that Camus invoked in the conclusion of *The Rebel*, when he celebrated the mentality of the south: "Historical absolutism, despite its triumph, has never ceased to come into collision with an irrepressible demand of human nature, of which the Mediterranean, where intelligence is intimately related to the blinding light of the sun, guards its secret."[29]

In the Mexican case, this southern outlook has taken a cultural form, the country's greatest achievement, according to Samuel Ramos, a mid twentieth-century essayist,[30] and a view echoed by a late twentieth-century American chronicler of the North American continent, emphasizing "the incredible kaleidoscope of its culture, an endlessly changing and fascinating spectrum of sights, sounds, and tastes," as the country's strength.[31]

All this would suggest a pattern of Mexican civilization significantly different from the American that dominates the rest of the continent. However, it seriously underestimates the influence that American values and popular culture have come to acquire in Mexico since World War II. Anglicisms, Hallowe'en, American football, credit cards, advertising, and supermarkets are some examples.[32] So too is a shift from a European-oriented to an American-based educational experience for Mexico's postwar elites.[33] One can note rock'n'roll's appeal to Mexican youth culture, in part as a reaction against the stifling quality of Mexican state nationalism,[34] and the role of American TV programs and films in helping make divorce, sexual freedom, youth rebellion, and drug use more acceptable.[35] Cross-border migration by tens of millions of American Latinos of Mexican origin has further reinforced the pattern. Civilizationally speaking, Mexico is closer to North American norms than at the time of the Mexican Revolution or of the country's independence. Yet, public opinion surveys show significantly lower levels of trust by Mexicans in their political institutions and in their fellow human beings than is true for Americans or Canadians.[36]

Is it possible to envisage a single, seamless North American civilization? Not by a long shot. The elements I have referred to in my discussion of the three countries show no signs of disappearing. The United States remains the Fortinbras of the continent, forging ahead in the quest for material abundance, technological prowess, and global reach, though with growing competition from Europe and East Asia within a geopolitical world beyond its unilateral control.[37] Canada is a would-be Fortinbras in the economic realm and has done well overall in developing its resource-based economy. (Staples are not a bad thing, if you have the right ones!) But Canada is a country marked by its European origins and not only by its North American location. And it is faced with the balancing act of keeping a multinational federation intact, something that ensures recurring crises around national unity. Hence, there is a more Hamlet-like feel to its political culture. Mexico has done reasonably well in surviving the encroachments of the nineteenth-century United States on its territory and resources. This is in no small part because culturally it has been more closely attuned to its pre-Columbian past, on the one hand, and to Latin America on the other; in its modern guise, it has remained a country with a less purely instrumental, market-driven mentality than either of its two northern neighbours. (Though here NAFTA and globalization are quickening the process of change.) At the same time, there is a deeply melancholic, nay tragic streak to the Mexican temperament that speaks of Hamlet and not of Fortinbras.

In sum, there can be no single North American civilization because temperamentally the three countries that make up the continent remain far apart.

Notes

1   Cited in John Harmon McElroy, *American Beliefs* (Chicago: Ivan Dee, 1999), 169.

2   Charles and Mary Beard, *The Rise of American Civilization* (New York: Macmillan, 1927).

3   Harold Laski, *The American Democracy* (New York: Viking, 1948), 397, 403.

4   Lerner, *America as a Civilization*, 60, 253.

5 Louis Hartz, *The Liberal Tradition in America,* in Hess, 160.

6 Theodore H. White, cited in Michael Lind, *The Next American Nation* (New York: Free Press, 1995), 220.

7 William James, *Pragmatism,* cited in Daniel H. Borus, *Twentieth Century Multiplicity: American Thought and Culture, 1900–1920* (Lanham: Rowman and Littlefield, 2009), 40.

8 Christopher Lasch, *The True and Only Heaven* (New York: Norton, 1991), 221.

9 Cited by Akash Kapur, "India is Getting All the Trappings of the New Century; But Is It Modern?," *New York Times* (July 29, 2010), http://www.nytimes.com/2010/07/30/world/asia/30iht-letter.html, accessed December 20, 2011.

10 Cited in Wolf Lepenies, *The Seduction of Culture in German History* (Princeton: Princeton University Press, 2006), 191–92.

11 Cf. Laski, *The American Democracy,* 27; Lerner, *America as a Civilization,* 253, 782.

12 Cf. Seymour Martin Lipset, *American Exceptionalism: A Double-Edged Sword* in Hess, 40.

13 Elliott, *Do the Americas Have a Common History?,* 40.

14 Daniel Boorstin and Brooks Mather Kelly, *A History of the United States* (New York: Prentice Hill, 1989): "American history is the story of a magic transformation. How did men and women from a tired Old World where people thought they knew what to expect become wide-eyed explorers of a New World…. What has been especially American about our ways of living and earning a living? Our ways of making war and peace? Our ways of worshipping God and fighting the Devil? Our ways of travelling and politicking, of building houses and cities?" cited in Hodgson, *The Myth of American Exceptionalism,* 98.

15 "Canada has been what the late H.A. Innis called a 'hard frontier.' The exploitation of her resources has required large accumulation of capital, corporate forms of business, and state support." S.D. Clark, *The Developing Canadian Community* (Toronto: University of Toronto Press, 1968), 248.

16 Sherrill Grace, *Canada and the Idea of North* (Montreal: McGill-Queen's University Press, 2002).

17 Maclure, *Quebec,* chap. 1.

18 Felipe Fernández-Armesto, *The Americas: A Hemispheric History* (New York: The Modern Library, 2003), 203–04.

19 Roger Bartra, *The Cage of Melancholy: Identity and Metamorphosis in the Mexican Character* (New Brunswick, NJ: Rutgers University Press, 1992), 80–81.

20 Monica de la Torre and Michael Wiegers, eds., "Introduction," *Reversible Monuments: Contemporary Mexican Poetry* (Port Townsend, WA: Copper Canyon Press, 2002), 7.

21 Nestor Garcia Canclini, *Hybrid Cultures* (Minneapolis: University of Minnesota Press, 1995), 132.

22 Shorris, *Life and Times of Mexico*, 711.

23 Lomnitz, *Death and the Idea of Mexico*, 23.

24 Bartra, *The Cage of Melancholy*, 33.

25 Alfonso Reyes, cited in Ramos, *Profile of Man and Culture in Mexico*, 75.

26 Paz, *Labyrinth of Solitude*, 22, 23.

27 Lomnitz, *Death and the Idea of Mexico*, 41.

28 Villegas, *American Extremes*, 33.

29 Albert Camus, "Thought at the Meridian," *The Rebel* (New York: Alfred Knopf, 1956), 300.

30 Ramos, *Profile of Man and Culture in Mexico*, 180, 194.

31 Anthony DePalma, *Here: A Biography of the New American Continent* (New York: Public Affairs, 2001), 161.

32 Meyer and Sherman, *The Course of Mexican History*, 711–12.

33 Camp, *Politics in Mexico*, 159.

34 Arthur Schmidt, "Making It Real Compared to What? Reconceptualizing Mexican History since 1940," in *Fragments of a Golden Age: Politics and Mexican Culture Since 1940*, ed. Gilbert Joseph et al. (Durham: Duke University Press, 2001), 48.

35 Riding, *Mexico*, 258.

36 Roderic Ai Camp, *Politics in Mexico: The Democratic Consolidation*, 5th ed. (New York: Oxford University Press, 2007), chap. 3.

37 Earl Fry, *Lament for America* (Toronto: University of Toronto Press, 2010), chap. 6.

TWELVE

Dwellers of the Labyrinth

"All the parts of the house are repeated many times, any place is another place.... The house is the same size as the world; or rather, it is the world."
Borges, *"The House of Asterion"*[1]

North America constitutes a labyrinth of identities. No one strain can describe it. Its multiple plates and perspectives include divisions between indigenous/non-indigenous, Protestant/Catholic/other, revolutionary/non-revolutionary, Spanish/English/French, great power/middle powers, and market societies/societies with pre-market characteristics.

What are the comparative lessons to be drawn from this book? All three North American countries had indigenous populations before Europeans arrived, and in all three indigenous peoples occupy marginal positions to this day. Is this simply a manifestation of colonialism and imperialism, a clash between civilizations in which those with the requisite antibodies along with superior economic, military, and organizational resources ultimately win out?[2] Or is there more to the tangled web of relations than corresponds to the simple dichotomy between conqueror and conquered? Appropriation, denial, greed, guilt, self-abnegation, and shame have all been part of the narrative, and there is no reason to believe that this will be any less true in the twenty-first century when international rights discourse looms larger than before and indigenous peoples often hold the key to crucial resource developments. In the words of Antonio Lamer, the Chief Justice of the Canadian Supreme Court at the time of the Delgamuukh decision in 1997 dealing with Aboriginal territorial rights, "Let us face it, we are all here to stay."[3]

The chosen people theme discussed in Chapter 2 is but one element in a larger picture. If the Protestant/Catholic divide were to be applied to the continent at large, then the real division of North America would be between the United States and English Canada on the one hand and Mexico and Quebec on the other. Fruitful comparisons can be drawn between the rugged individualism, church pluralism, representative political institutions, and strong work ethic associated with Protestantism and the more hierarchical forms of ecclesiastical, political, and social organization associated with Catholicism. After all, Max Weber, the first theorist of the Protestantism-capitalism nexus, acquired some of his intuitions during a lengthy stay in the United States in 1904. Mexico and Quebec were not at the forefront of capitalist development, mass popular education and literacy, or democratic empowerment in North America. They adhered to these subsequently, and some of their "relative backwardness" may well have had its roots in this earlier religious divide.

The native languages of North America's peoples are many, but three European-derived ones have come to dominate in the contemporary era. Each had to adapt and change to meet the altered circumstances of New World societies. Once again, the relevant division is between the United States and English Canada on the one hand, and Mexico and Quebec on the other. The position that English has acquired on the continent and beyond is a direct reflection of the hegemonic position that the United States—and with it American English—has come to enjoy, with English Canada something of a camp follower. This is not to suggest that either French or Spanish is under imminent threat of disappearing in Quebec or Mexico, even if the population of francophones in North America is barely 6 per cent that of hispanophones. But the centrality of the United States to the continent—constituting some two-thirds of its total population—and the manifest attraction and influence it has had culturally, economically, militarily, and politically on its two neighbours renders French and Spanish far more subject to the influence of English in North America than the other way around. The *lingua franca* of the labyrinth is not Esperanto!

When it comes to survival or *la survivance*, Canada and Mexico are similar. National identities may be fragile and changing, but for a number of reasons it is the two smaller countries that have had to worry persistently about co-existing with a mastodon of a neighbour, one moreover that had a voracious appetite for expansion back in the nineteenth century. The foreign and domestic policies of both countries have been inordinately influenced by keeping the relationship with the United States on an even keel. By comparison, both Canada and Mexico have rarely occupied a central place in American decision-making, which is far more concerned with internal priorities or with any perceived external menace to its own imperial sway. In the words of a French ambassador to the United States in the early part of the twentieth century, underlining American geopolitical supremacy on the North American continent, "On the north, she has a weak neighbour; on the south, another weak neighbour; on the east, fish; and on the west, fish."[4]

Like Ariadne's thread, capitalism runs through the North American labyrinth. Feudalism had its hold in an earlier phase of Mexican development, and the *seigneuries* along the St. Lawrence River bespoke the legacy of New France. But the mercantile spirit was front and centre of the American experience, despite the slave-based southern economy, and that spirit has come to dominate the continent as a whole. The Canada-United States Free Trade Agreement followed by NAFTA are its modern consecration, supposedly uniting the continent through the free flow of capital and commerce. Obstacles to the full realization of this vision have not been lacking—e.g., strong protectionist pressures from loggers, truckers, and farmers—with national security preoccupations following 9/11 a further significant kink along the way. The real challenge for North America, however, is to go beyond a purely market-driven vision of the continent to one in which cultural, environmental, and social cohesion are the other side of economic efficacy. The double-dip economic recession that the world economy is experiencing at the moment, coupled with the right-wing turn in public policy in all three countries, makes any vision of a more socially oriented North America something of a utopian one. But no economic credo lasts forever, as the fall of communism teaches us, and the tooth-in-claw version of capitalism that neo-liberalism has been propagating over the past three decades, much like the Gilded Age in American politics of the late nineteenth century, will also have its comeuppance. Then perhaps an element of solidarity, so sadly missing in the original NAFTA arrangements, will become a possibility.

Democracy in its representative form took root in North America long before it was established in most of the Old World. The continent was spared the versions of dictatorship associated with twentieth-century totalitarianisms of both the Right and Left. Mexico has had closer encounters with authoritarianism than its two northern neighbours, though its most recent experience has made it a genuine multi-party state. As a result, there is a better political fit among the three North American countries today than at any previous time in their histories—not that democratic institutions at the national level necessarily translate into a sense of shared identity at the continental, as the current travails of the European Union would underline. But they at least make possible a heightened dialogue across national lines and a sense of potential common interests between ordinary citizens and between broadly based associational groups.

All three North American countries, as befits newly settled societies, have at various junctures used the state as an instrument of nation-building. Canada and Mexico have also had recourse to the state as an instrument of defensive nationalism against the United States, especially in the cultural and economic spheres. The United States and Canada developed a reasonably effective tax state over time, though the American one, because of deep internal political divisions, seems far less able to cope with its current debt crisis than the Canadian. Mexico, for its part, still has quite some distance to go before it is able to collect the requisite revenues to fund a minimal welfare state. In this respect, its fiscal situation resembles that of countries such as Italy or Greece, where massive tax fraud by the citizenry, especially the well-heeled, is the norm. The United States, as befits a great power with far-flung world interests, has a far more developed military and security apparatus than the two other countries—too costly, as a number of intelligent critics have pointed out.[5] In certain areas, such as anti-trust policy, food and drug legislation, or the environment, the American state has historically had a more developed regulatory capacity than Canada or Mexico. When it comes to overall social expenditure, however, Canada is closer to the northern European welfare state model than either of the other two countries. So, diversity rather than uniformity characterizes North American attitudes toward the state.

Federalism is a shared characteristic of all three countries, something truer of North America than of any other multi-state continent. The Americans pioneered in this regard, with both Mexico and Canada following suit. The division of powers between centre and constituent units has not been identical in the three countries, and there have been significant shifts in the relative strengths of central governments versus constituent units at various times in each country's history. Mexican federalism went into something of an eclipse during the long period of PRI ascendancy in the twentieth century, but it is very much a part of the present reality of the country.[6] Canadians and Americans, in thinking about comparative federalism, would do well to expand their horizons to include Mexico in their accounts.

Utopian expectations surrounded the discovery and first explorations of the New World. Many of these were to be disappointed, as successive El Doradas proved to be something of a mirage and as human nature did not turn out to be noticeably different in the New World than in the Old. What characterized the United States in particular was a greater belief in the possibility of remaking the world anew, of shaking off the bonds of the past and embracing the unfamiliar and the untried. Canada and Mexico, by comparison, retained stronger features of their European colonial pasts—Spanish, French, British as the case might be—and these have coloured their political and cultural development. Not surprisingly, something of this attitude also carries over into views of the originality of one's civilization. The Americans have been far bolder in staking claims to constitute a new civilization, and observers from Europe and beyond have eagerly egged them on. By that standard, the two other North American states have been pale reflections of the American civilizational sun. Or, more accurately, Canada has retained a greater openness to European values than the United States, as has Mexico, which like other Latin American countries has received its cultural structure, language, religion, customs, and conception of life from Europe.[7]

There is much to be gained from mapping comparisons and differences among the three North American countries. But however stimulating the exercise may prove, we still face hard questions about what might bind North America together. So here are my concluding thoughts.

Recognition of being part of the New World is the *sina qua non* of North American identity. It is shared by the inhabitants of all three North American countries—and, indeed, by those of the Caribbean and Central and South America as well. Some came to adopt these New World identities easily, others with greater reluctance, still others by merging old identities with new in a mosaic that was to become the basis for newly established national identities.

Visions of the founders or settlers of post-Conquest North American societies were not confined to the geographical lines they knew in their day. Nueva España stretched down into Central America and northwards into Texas, the American Southwest, and California. Navigators such as Juan de Fuca and Juan Francisco de la Bodega y Quadra explored the coast of the Pacific Northwest, including British Columbia. For his part, Thomas Jefferson was one of many Americans to take the entire continent as his country's eventual domain. The French empire in the New World once reached from the St. Lawrence through to the Great Lakes and down the Mississippi to New Orleans. And the Fathers of Canadian Confederation had a continent-wide vision of a country in mind, not the crimped 1867 dimensions of Canada's four founding provinces.

North Americans have seldom thought of themselves as sharing a common destiny, but at times their destinies have been intimately interwoven. The American War of Independence was to have a long-term impact on both Canada and Mexico. The Mexican-American War left huge chunks of formerly Mexican territory under the American flag. The two world wars brought about closer Canadian-American relations in the military and diplomatic arenas. The Mexican Revolution, for its part, saw initial American entanglement in Mexican affairs followed by greater disengagement in the 1930s and 1940s. The Cold War reinforced Canada-United States integration, economically, militarily, and politically, symbolized in the building of the DEW (Distant Early Warning radar lines) in northern Canada and bilateral agreements such as NORAD. The Canada-United States Auto Pact of 1964, followed by the trade agreements of 1988 and 1994, all spoke to greater continental economic integration.

Migration patterns over time also reflect North American-wide currents. The Underground Railway in the nineteenth century, American draft dodgers in the 1960s, and Americans fleeing Bush and neo-conservatism in the early years of this century saw Canada at the receiving end of American immigration. To such migrants, Canada appeared as a softer, less Hobbesian version of the North American dream. Conversely, large numbers of Canadians, from textile and other factory workers in the nineteenth century to academics, other professionals, and actors in the twentieth and twenty-first, have migrated to the United States in search of job and career opportunities. For them, the United States is the land where entrepreneurship reigns and personal aspirations, less easily attained back home, can be realized.

The same has been true for Mexican migrants fleeing poverty over the past century and a half, both the Braceros of an earlier period and the millions crossing to *el otro lado* (the other side) in our day. According to the American Census Bureau, there are 12 million people in the United States who were born in Mexico. This amounts to more than 10 per cent of the Mexican population in Mexico.[8]

Conversely, Mexico has been a country of choice for Americans, and more recently Canadians, seeking temporary escape from winter and a harsh northern climate or lured by the cadences of a society where vanished gods once dwelled and traces of an ancient past are there for the finding. In this respect, the appeal of Mexico resembles the fascination of Greece, Italy, or Spain for northern Europeans.

What may become more apparent with time is the importance of deeper continental ties in an era of globalization and shrinking resources. Perhaps, in a break with the trade-driven NAFTA framework, which has experienced something of an impasse in recent years, we can begin to envision North America as a cultural space with many shades. Somewhat greater cultural symbiosis may yet emerge, for example, through the Latino impact on the United States and not just the other way around; through intellectual interchange between universities, research institutes, journals, and publications; and through a recognition of the quite distinct place that each of the three countries occupies in North America. Canada is something of the continent's Scandinavia with its mixed economy, a tax state that works, and a reasonable approximation of the welfare state. (Quebec fits the rubric even better than the rest of Canada, with less income inequality than Ontario, Alberta, or British Columbia.[9]) The United States as the major North American power combines some of the characteristics of European great powers—Britain, France, Germany, and Russia all rolled into one—with its cultural dynamism, economic virtuosity, imperial reach, and military prowess. Mexico is the Mediterranean of North America with a physical landscape combining austerity, lushness, and a lingering legacy of the past.

North America has been a continent of political stability for close to a century in a world that has known deep ideological divides. It is a continent with continuing population exchange, both legal and illegal, as well as immigration from around the world, and the hybridity and fusion this gives rise to. This is a continent whose inhabitants share many of the civilizational norms of open, future-oriented, technologically driven societies, albeit with important residues from the Old World (such as religion and social values) colouring behaviour as well.

Catastrophic events may generate their own sense of shared fate. Oil spills in the Gulf of Mexico or in the Arctic, earthquakes and tsunamis along the Cascadian Fault, weather disruptions caused by El Niño and la Niña, crop failures, and devastating hurricanes do not respect political boundaries, and reactions to them may similarly cross national lines. The fall-out from the narco-trafficking wars is not limited to the northern and western states of Mexico. This may be a dystopian view of how unity is forged, but sadly it is often the most realistic. After all, the legacy of a century of wars and the depredations that accompanied them had much to do with the forging of closer ties among France, Germany, and other European countries after 1945 and led to the establishment of the European Union.

Though a North American Union is most definitely *not* on the agenda, this does not foreclose a greater sense of common interests among the continent's inhabitants. This is more likely within overlapping border regions where common economic interests and population intermixing have occurred. It may also prove true at the larger continental level. What should matter is that we are all New World societies, that we all were once colonized by European empires, that the languages we speak and the religions we profess (or do not profess) were Old World in origin, that our economic and political institutions are not antithetical to one another, and that we share many civilizational traits and a common geographical space.

The construct that may be relevant here is that of nested identities. Just as the primary identity of most indigenous peoples in North America may be their indigenous one, they are also citizens of their respective three countries and therefore Canadians, Americans, or Mexicans as well. In similar fashion, francophone Québécois may feel their primary identity to be Québécois, but they are bearers of a Canadian one at the same time. There are regional identities in all three countries that co-exist with larger national loyalties, not always in harmonious fashion, as the American Civil War reminds us. Nation-states do not have a monopoly on the constituent identities of their citizens, despite the salience that nation-states have acquired in the international system.

To define themselves as North Americans would not be the first choice of the overwhelming majority of the continent's inhabitants. Nor is it likely to become so in the decades to come. But in a globalized world, where continental (or sub-continental) ensembles loom larger than before, the notion of being a North American (as well as a Mexican, American, and Canadian) is not stretching the limits of the feasible. It can become one of the identities one assumes, alongside the local, the regional, and the national. In that sense, being a North American can be nested in these other overlapping forms of identity.

Can the inhabitants of North America begin to acquire some of the accoutrements of a shared "North Americanness"? The answer to this question is by no means yes. But in a multipolar world where the United States is no longer the superpower it once was, and at a time when a genuine multilateralism comes to characterize its outlook on the world, the attitudes of its two neighbours to initiatives further linking the three countries and their peoples may turn out to be quite positive. The prophets of such a North American vision will not be the trade negotiators and Wall Street insiders who have dominated the discourse until now, but artists and story-tellers, netizens and ecologists, indigenous peoples and their non-indigenous counterparts who come to articulate, at a deeper cultural, nay existential level, a sense of sharing a common living space. Then, perhaps, we will be able to imagine Quetzalcoatl's return.

Notes

1 Jorge Luis Borges, "The House of Asterion," *Labyrinths: Selected Stories and Other Writings* (New York: New Directions, 1964), 139.

2 Ian Morris, *Why the West Rules—For Now: The Patterns of History and What They Reveal about the Future* (New York: Farrar, Straus and Giroux, 2010).

3 Canada, Supreme Court, *Delgamuukh vs. British Columbia*, [1997], 3 S.C.R. 1010, #186.

4 Jules Jusserand, French Ambassador to the United States from 1902 to 1925, cited by Fry, *Lament for America*, 78.

5 Andrew Bacevich, *The Limits of Power: The End of American Exceptionalism* (New York: Metropolitan Books, 2008); see also, Fry, *Lament for America*.

6 Cf. Mariano Palacios Alcocer, ed., *Federalismo y relaciones intergubernamentales* (Mexico: Senado de la Republica, 2003); Alicia Hernandez Chavez, "Federalismo y Gobernabilidad en México," in *Federalismos latinoamericanos: México/ Brasil/Argentina*, ed. Marcello Carmagnani (Mexico: El Colegio de México, 1993), 263–99.

7 Zea, "The Actual Function of Philosophy in Latin America," 361, 363; also Gilberto Freyre, *New World in the Tropics: The Culture of Modern Brazil* (New York: Knopf, 1959), 219–22.

8 Weintraub, *Unequal Partners*, 98.

9 Paul Bernard and Hicham Raiq, "Le Québec est-il une société égalitaire?," *L'État du Québec 2011*, ed. Miriam Fahmy (Montreal: Boréal, 2011), 55–57.

Bibliography

Adams, Brooks. *The New Empire*. New York: Macmillan, 1902.

Adams, Michael. *Unlikely Utopia: The Surprising Triumph of Canadian Pluralism*. Toronto: Viking, 2007.

Aitken, Hugh. "Defensive Expansionism: The State and Economic Growth in Canada." In *Approaches to Canadian Economic History*, ed. W.T. Easterbrook and Mel Watkins. 183–221. Toronto: Carleton Library, 1967.

Ajzenstat, Janet, et al., eds. *Canada's Founding Debates*. Toronto: University of Toronto Press, 2003.

Alcocer, Mariano Palacios, ed. *Federalismo y relaciones intergubernamentales*. Mexico: Senado de la Republica, 2003.

Alonso, Jorge. "Democracia y Nuevos Municipios." In *La remunicipalizacion de Chiapas*, ed. X.L. Solano and A.B. Cal y Mayor. 355–68. Mexico: Porrua, 2007.

Appleby, Joyce. *Capitalism and a New Social Order: The Republican Vision of the 1790s*. New York: New York University Press, 1984.

Appleby, Joyce. *Liberalism and Republicanism in the Historical Imagination*. Cambridge, MA: Harvard University Press, 1992.

Appleby, Joyce. *The Relentless Revolution: A History of Capitalism*. New York: Norton, 2010.

Archer, Robin. *Why is There No Labor Party in the United States?* Princeton: Princeton University Press, 2007.

Arciniegas, German. *Latin America: A Cultural History*. New York: Knopf, 1966.

Arrighi, Giovanni. *Adam Smith in Beijing*. London: Verso, 2007.

Audet, Noël. *Entre la Boussole et l'Étoile.* Montreal: XYZ, 2006.

Bacevich, Andrew. *The Limits of Power: The End of American Exceptionalism.* New York: Metropolitan Books, 2008.

Baida, Peter. *Poor Richard's Legacy: American Business Values from Benjamin Franklin to Donald Trump.* New York: W. Morrow, 1990.

Bailey, David C. *¡Viva Cristo Rey! The Cristero Rebellion and the Church-State Conflict in Mexico.* Austin: University of Texas Press, 1974.

Bailey, Thomas A. "Theodore Roosevelt and the Alaska Boundary Settlement." *Canadian Historical Review* 28, no. 2 (June 1937): 123–30.

Bailyn, Bernard. *The Ideological Origins of the American Revolution.* Cambridge, MA: Harvard University Press, 1967.

BBC. "Free Market Flawed, Says Survey." November 9, 2009. http://news.bbc.co.uk/2/hi/in_depth/8347409.stm. Accessed May 20, 2011.

Baldwin, Neil. *Legends of the Plumed Serpent: Biography of a Mexican God.* New York: Public Affairs, 1998.

Baritz, Louis. *City on a Hill.* New York: John Wiley, 1964.

Barman, Jean. *The West beyond the West: A History of British Columbia.* 3rd ed. Toronto: University of Toronto Press, 2007.

Bartels, Larry. *Unequal Democracy: The Political Economy of the New Gilded Age.* Princeton: Princeton University Press, 2008.

Bartra, Roger. *The Cage of Melancholy: Identity and Metamorphosis in the Mexican Character.* New Brunswick, NJ: Rutgers University Press, 1992.

Beard, Charles, and Mary Beard. *The Rise of American Civilization.* New York: Macmillan, 1927.

Bellah, Robert, et al. *Habits of the Heart: Individualism and Commitment in American Life.* New York: Harper and Row, 1986.

Bellah, Robert N., and Steven M. Tipton, eds. *The Robert Bellah Reader.* Durham: Duke University Press, 2006.

Bercovitch, Sacvan. *The American Jeremiad.* Madison: University of Wisconsin Press, 1978.

Bercovitch, Sacvan. "The American Jeremiad." In *American Social and Political Thought: A Concise Introduction,* ed. Andreas Hess. 80–88. Edinburgh: Edinburgh University Press, 2000.

Berger, Carl. *The Sense of Power.* Toronto: University of Toronto Press, 1970.

Berkhofer, Robert, Jr. *The White Man's Indian.* New York: Vintage, 1979.

Bernard, Paul, and Hicham Raïq. "Le Quebec est-il une société égalitaire." In *L'État du Québec 2011,* ed. Miriam Fahmy. 49-69. Montreal: Boréal, 2011.

Bitab, Karim, and Robert Fadel, eds. *Regards sur la France.* Paris: Seuil, 2007.

Blackshaw, Tony. *Zygmunt Bauman*. Milton Park: Routledge, Key Sociologists. 2005.

Blancarte, Roberto. "Religion, Church, and State." In *Changing Structure of Mexico*, ed. Laura Randall. 424–37. Armonk, NY: Sharpe, 2006.

Bolaño, Roberto. *2666*. New York: Farrar, Straus and Giroux, 2008.

Boorstin, Daniel, and Brooks Mather Kelly. *A History of the United States*. New York: Prentice Hill, 1989.

Borges, Jorge Luis. *Labyrinths: Selected Stories and Other Writings*. New York: New Directions, 1964.

Borus, Daniel H. *Twentieth Century Multiplicity: American Thought and Culture, 1900–1920*. Lanham: Rowman and Littlefield, 2009.

Bouchard, Gérard. *The Making of the Nations and Cultures of the New World*. Montreal: McGill-Queen's University Press, 2008.

Brading, D.A. *Mexican Phoenix: Our Lady of Guadalupe*. Cambridge: Cambridge University Press, 2001.

Brands, H.W. *American Colossus: The Triumph of Capitalism, 1865–1900*. New York: Doubleday, 2010.

Brebner, John. *North Atlantic Triangle: The Interplay of Canada, the United States and Great Britain*. Toronto: Carleton Library, 1968.

Brinton, Laurel J., and Margery Fee. "Canadian English." In *The Cambridge History of the English Language*, Vol. VI, *English in North America*, ed. John Algeo. 422–40. Cambridge: Cambridge University Press, 2001.

Brooks, Stephen. *America through Foreign Eyes*. Toronto: Oxford University Press, 2002.

Brouwer, Ruth Compton. "Canadian Protestant Overseas Missions." In *Empires of Religion*, ed. Hilary Carey. 288–310. London: Palgrave, 2008.

Bryan, William Jennings. "No Cross of Gold." Address to the National Democratic Convention, July 9, 1896. http://projects.vassar.edu/1896/crossofgold.html. Accessed Dec. 19, 2011.

Buffington, Robert, and William French. "The Culture of Modernity." In *The Oxford History of Mexico*, ed. Michael Meyer and William Beezley. Chap. 13. New York: Oxford University Press, 2000.

Burtless, Gary, and Ron Haskins. "Inequality, Economic Mobility, and Social Policy." In Schuck and Wilson, *Understanding America*, 495–538.

Camp, Roderic Ai. *Mexico's Mandarins: Crafting a Power Elite for the 21st Century*. Berkeley: University of California Press, 2002.

Camp, Roderic Ai. *Politics in Mexico: The Democratic Consolidation*. 5th ed. New York: Oxford University Press, 2007.

Camus, Albert. *The Rebel*. New York: Alfred Knopf, 1956.

Canada, House of Commons. *Special Committee on Radio Broadcasting: Minutes and Proceedings of Evidence*. Ottawa: F.A. Aclaud, 1932.

Canada. Supreme Court. *Delgamuukh vs. British Columbia*, [1997], 3 S.C.R. 1010.

Canclini, Nestor Garcia. *Hybrid Cultures*. Minneapolis: University of Minnesota Press, 1995.

Careless, Maurice. "Limited Identities in Canada." *Canadian Historical Review* 50, no. 1 (1969): 1–10. http://dx.doi.org/10.3138/CHR-050-01-01.

Carrasco, Salvador. "The Invisible Sight." In *The Zapatista Reader,* ed. Tom Hayden. 166–77. New York: Nation Books, 2002.

Chandler, Alfred D. "The Role of Business in the United States: A Historical Survey." *Daedelus* 98 (Winter 1969): 23–40.

Chavez, Alicia Hernandez. "Federalismo y Gobernabilidad en México." In *Federalismos latinoamericanos: México/Brasil/Argentina*, ed. Marcello Carmagnani. 263–99. Mexico: El Colegio de México, 1993.

Cherry, Conrad, ed., *God's New Israel: Religious Interpretations of American Destiny*. Chapel Hill: University of North Carolina Press, 1998.

Clark, S.D. *The Developing Canadian Community*. Toronto: University of Toronto Press, 1968.

Confer, Clarissa W. *Daily Life during the Indian Wars*. Santa Barbara: Greenwood, 2011.

Corbo, Claude. *Encyclopedia of French Canadian Cultural Heritage in North America*. http://www.ameriquefrancaise.org/en/article-466/Alexis_de_Tocqueville%E2%80%99s_visit_to_Lower_Canada_in_1831.html. Accessed May 20, 2011.

Crane, Hart. *The Bridge: Quaker Hill*. http://www.poetryfoundation.org/poem/172033. Accessed May 20, 2011.

Creighton, Donald. *Harold Adams Innis, Portrait of a Scholar*. Toronto: University of Toronto Press, 1957.

de Crèvecoeur, M.G.J. *Letters from an American Farmer*. Philadelphia: Matthew Carey, 1793. http://xroads.virginia.edu/~hyper/crev/letter03.html. Accessed December 18, 2011.

Cumings, Bruce. *Dominion from Sea to Sea: Pacific Ascendancy and American Power*. New Haven: Yale University Press, 2009.

Curzio, Leonardo. "La Transicíon a la Democracia y la Construccíon de Ciudadania en México." In *La democracia en América Latina, Un Barco a la Deriva*, ed. Waldo Ansaldi. 313–31. Buenos Aires: Fundo de Cultural Economica, 2006.

Davis, Mike. *Planet of Slums*. London: Verso, 2006.

Delden, Maarten von. *Carlos Fuentes, Mexico, and Modernity*. Nashville: Vanderbilt University Press, 1993.

DePalma, Anthony. *Here: A Biography of the New American Continent*. New York: Public Affairs, 2001.

Didion, Joan. *Where I Was From*. New York: Knopf, 2003.

Diggins, John Patrick. *The Promise of Pragmatism*. Chicago: University of Chicago Press, 1994.

Dilke, Oswald, and Margaret Dilke, "The Adjustment of Ptolemaic Atlases to Feature the New World." In Haase and Reinhold, *The Classical Tradition and the Americas*, 117–34.

Dorman, Robert L. "The Regionalist Movement in America." In Wilson, *The New Regionalism*, 1–17.

Economist. "Onwards and Upwards." December 19, 2009: 37–40.

Elliott, J.H. *Do the Americas Have a Common History?* Providence: John Carter Brown Library, 1996.

Engler, Berndt, and Oliver Scheiding, eds. *A Companion to American Cultural History: From the Colonial Period to the End of the 19th Century*. Trier: WVT Wissenschaftlicher Verlag Trier, 2009.

Erichsen, Gerald. "Spanglish: English's Assault on Spanish." http://spanish.about.com/cs/historyofspanish/a/spanglish.htm. Accessed May 20, 2011.

Evans, Sterling, ed. *The Borderlands of the Canadian and American Wests*. Lincoln: University of Nebraska Press, 2006.

Everwine, Peter. *Working the Song Fields: Poems of the Aztecs*. Spokane: Eastern Washington. University Press, 2009.

Faulkner, William. *Requiem for a Nun*. New York: Random House, 1951.

Fernández-Armesto, Felipe. *The Americas: A Hemispheric History*. New York: The Modern Library, 2003.

Fischer, Claude. *Made in America: A Social History of American Culture and Character*. Chicago: University of Chicago Press, 2010.

Fischer, David Hackett. *Albion's Seed: Four British Folkways in America*. New York: Oxford University Press, 1989.

Fischer, David Hackett. *Champlain's Dream*. New York: Simon and Schuster, 2008.

Fishman, Joshua A. *European Vernacular Literacy: A Sociolinguistic and Historical Introduction*. Bristol: Multilingual Matters, 2010.

Foner, Philip, ed. *The Complete Writings of Thomas Paine*. New York: The Citadel Press, 1945.

Fowler, Will, and Peter Lambert, eds. *Political Violence and the Construction of National Identity in Latin America*. New York: Palgrave Macmillan, 2006. http://dx.doi.org/10.1057/9780230601727.

Fox, Jeremy, "Mexnarcos," *Open Democracy*, January 17, 2011. http://www.opendemocracy.net/jeremy-fox/mexnarcos. Accessed December 18, 2011.

Foxley, Alejandro. "More Market or More State for Latin America?" In Mainwaring and Scully, *Democratic Governance in Latin America*, 129–54.

Francis, Douglas, and Chris Kitzan, eds. *The Prairie West as Promised Land*. Calgary: University of Calgary Press, 2007.

Friesen, John W., and Virginia Lyons Friesen. *The Palgrave Companion to North American Utopias*. London: Macmillan, 2004.

Freyre, Gilberto. *New World in the Tropics: The Culture of Modern Brazil*. New York: Knopf, 1959.

Fry, Earl. *Lament for America*. Toronto: University of Toronto Press, 2010.

Frye, Northrop. *The Bush Garden: Essays on the Canadian Imagination*. Toronto: Anansi, 1971.

Fuentes, Carlos. *The Buried Mirror: Reflections on Spain and the New World*. Boston: Houghton Miflin Harcourt, 1999.

Fuentes, Carlos. *A New Time for Mexico*. New York: Farrar, Straus and Giroux, 1996.

Funes, Patricia. *Salvar la nacion*. Buenos Aires: Prometeo Libros, 2006.

Galbraith, James. *The Predator State: How Conservatives Abandoned the Market and Why Liberals Should Too*. New York: The Free Press, 2008.

Gapper, John. Review of *American Colossus: The Triumph of Capitalism, 1865–1900*, by H.W. Brands. *Financial Times*, December 17, 2010: 10.

Gibler, John. *Mexico Unconquered: Chronicles of Power and Revolt*. San Francisco: City Lights, 2009.

Gibler, John. "Teacher Rebellion in Oaxaca." *In These Times*, August 21, 2006. http://www.inthesetimes.com/article/2795/. Accessed December 20, 2011.

Gilchrist, Brent. *Cultus Americus: Varieties of the Liberal Tradition in American Political Culture, 1600–1865*. Lanham: Lexington, 2006.

Globe and Mail. "Canadian Centre for Policy Alternatives Study." April 8, 2010: 4.

Goethe, Johann Wolfgang von. "America, you've got it better." http://davidsbuendler.freehostia.com/america.htm. Accessed May 20, 2011.

Goetz, Rainer. *La lengua Española: Panorama Sociohistórico*. Jefferson, NC: McFarland, 2007.

Grace, Sherrill. *Canada and the Idea of North*. Montreal: McGill-Queen's University Press, 2002.

Grayson, George. *Mexican Messiah: Andrés Manuel Lopez Obrador*. University Park, PA: Pennsylvania State University Press, 2007.

Guardian Weekly. "First Americans Come Last." January 29, 2010: 25–27.

Haase, Wolfgang, and Meyer Reinhold, eds. *The Classical Tradition and the Americas*. Vol. 1: *European Images of the Americas and the Classical Tradition*. Berlin/New York: de Gruyter, 1994.

Halpern, David. *The Hidden Wealth of Nations*. Cambridge: Polity, 2010.

Hanke, Lewis, ed. *Do the Americas Have a Common History? A Critique of the Bolton Thesis*. New York: Knopf, 1964.

Hartz, Louis. "The Nature of Revolution," *Society* 42, no. 4 (2005 [1968]): 54–61.

Hatch, Nathan. "The Democratization of Christianity and the Character of American Politics." In *Religion and American Politics*. 2nd ed., ed. Mark Noll and Luke Harlow. 92–120. New York: Oxford University Press, 2007. http://dx.doi.org/10.1093/acprof:oso/9780195317145.003.0006.

Hegel, Georg. *Philosophy of History*. New York: Cosimo Classics, 2007.

Herrero, Beatriz Fernández. *La Utopía de América*. Barcelona: Anthropos, 1992.

Hess, Andreas, ed. *American Social and Political Thought: A Concise Introduction*. Edinburgh: Edinburgh University Press, 2000.

High, Steven. "The Narcissism of Small Differences—Canadian English." In Magda Fahrni and Robert Rutherdale, eds. *Creating Postwar Canada*. 89–110. Vancouver: University of British Columbia Press, 2008.

Hodgson, Godfrey. *The Myth of American Exceptionalism*. New Haven: Yale University Press, 2009.

Horowitz, Gad. "Conservatism, Liberalism, and Socialism in Canada: An Interpretation." *Canadian Journal of Economics and Political Science* 32, no. 2 (1966): 143–71. http://dx.doi.org/10.2307/139794.

Howe, Daniel Walker. *What Hath God Wrought: The Transformation of America 1815–1848*. New York: Oxford University Press, 2007.

Huber, Evelyn, and John Stephens. "Successful Social Policy Regimes?" In Mainwaring and Scully, *Democratic Governance in Latin America*, 155–209.

Iguiniz, Margarita Estrada, and Pascal Labazee, eds. *Globalización y localidad: espacios, actores, movilidades e identidades*. Mexico: Ciesas, 2007.

Innis, Harold. *The Fur Trade in Canada*. Rev. ed. Toronto: University of Toronto Press, 1970.

Jacobs, Lawrence, and Theda Skocpol, eds. *Inequality and American Democracy.* New York: Russell Sage Foundation, 2005.

Jantti, Markus, Knut Roed, Robin Naylor, et al. *"American Exceptionalism in a New Light: A Comparison of Intergenerational Earnings Mobility in the Nordic Countries, the United Kingdom and the United States."* IZA Discussion Paper No. 1938, January 2006. ftp://repec.iza.org/RePEc/Discussionpaper/dp1938.pdf.

Jefferson, Thomas. First Inaugural Address. http://www.bartleby.com/124/pres16.html. Accessed December 20, 2011.

Joseph, Gilbert, et al., eds. *Fragments of a Golden Age: Politics and Mexican Culture since 1940.* Durham: Duke University Press, 2001.

Joseph, Gilbert, and Timothy Henderson, eds. *The Mexico Reader: History, Culture, Politics.* Durham: Duke University Press, 2002.

Judt, Tony. *Postwar: A History of Europe since 1945.* New York: Penguin, 2005.

Kaag, John Jacob. "Pragmatism and the Lessons of Experience." *Daedalus* 138, no. 2 (Spring 2009): 63–72. http://dx.doi.org/10.1162/daed.2009.138.2.63.

Kagan, Robert. *Dangerous Nation.* New York: Knopf, 2006.

Kammen, Michael. *A Season of Youth: The American Revolution and the Historical Imagination.* New York: Knopf, 1978.

Kapur, Akash. "India is Getting All the Trappings of the New Century; But Is It Modern?" *New York Times,* July 29, 2010. http://www.nytimes.com/2010/07/30/world/asia/30iht-letter.html. Accessed December 20, 2011.

Keen, Benjamin. *The Aztec Image in Western Thought.* New Brunswick, NJ: Rutgers University Press, 1971.

Keister, Lisa A. *Wealth in America: Trends in Wealth Inequality.* New York: Cambridge University Press, 2000. http://dx.doi.org/10.1017/CBO9780511625503.

Kilbourn, William, ed. *Canada: A Guide to the Peaceable Kingdom.* Toronto: Macmillan, 1970.

Kimmage, Michael. "The Hands that Built the Conservative Movement." *Dissent* (August 2009). http://www.dissentmagazine.org/online.php?id=281. Accessed December 20, 2011.

Kipling, Rudyard. *American Notes,* "At the Golden Gate." 1891. http://www.gutenberg.org/files/977/977-h/977-h.htm. Accessed December 20, 2011.

Kohn, Edward. *This Kindred People: Canadian-American Relations and the Anglo-Saxon Idea, 1895–1903.* Montreal: McGill-Queen's University Press, 2004.

Konrad, Victor, and Heather Nicol. *Beyond Walls: Re-inventing the Canada-United States Borderlands*. Aldershot: Ashgate, 2008.

Krauze, Enrique. *Mexico: Biography of Power*. New York: Harper Collins, 1997.

Lafaye, Jacques. *Quetzalcoatl and Guadalupe: The Formation of Mexican National Consciousness 1531–1813*. Chicago: University of Chicago Press, 1987.

Lalonde, Michèle. *Speak White*. Trans. Albert Herring. Albert Herring Everything Website. http://everything2.com/user/Albert+Herring/writeups/Speak+White. Accessed May 20, 2011.

"Land God Gave to Cain." *The Canadian Encyclopedia*. http://www.thecanadianencyclopedia.com/index.cfm?PgNm=TCE&Params=A1A RTA0004499. Accessed December 18, 2011.

Lapierre, André. "Parcours toponymiques de l'Amérique française." In *Langue, espace, société*, ed. Claude Poirier. 227–35. Ste. Foy: Presses de l'Université Laval, 1994.

Laponce, Jean. *Languages and Their Territories*. Toronto: University of Toronto Press, 1987.

Lasch, Christopher. *The True and Only Heaven*. New York: Norton, 1991.

Laski, Harold. *The American Democracy*. New York: Viking, 1948.

Leon-Portilla, Miguel. *The Ancient Mexicans through their Stories and Songs*. Mexico: Fondo de Cultura, 1961.

Leon-Portilla, Miguel. *Mesoamerica 1492, and on the Eve of 1992*. University of Maryland Working Papers, Department of Spanish and Portuguese, No. 1, 1988.

Leonhardt, David. "In Health Bill, Obama Attacks Wealth Inequality," *New York Times*, March 23, 2010. Accessed December 20, 2011.

Lepenies, Wolf. *The Seduction of Culture in German History*. Princeton: Princeton University Press, 2006.

Lerner, Max. *American as a Civilization*. New York: Simon and Schuster, 1957.

Levitt, Kari. *Silent Surrender: The Multinational Corporation in Canada*. Toronto: Macmillan, 1970.

Lida, David. *First Stop in the New World: Mexico City, the Capital of the 21st Century*. New York: Penguin, 2009.

Limerick, Patricia Nelson. "The Realization of the American West." In Wilson, *The New Regionalism*, 71–98.

Lincoln, Abraham. "Address to New Jersey State Senate." February 21, 1861. http://teachingamericanhistory.org/library/index.asp?document-1062. Accessed December 18, 2011.

Lincoln, Abraham. "The Gettysburg Address." http://showcase.netins.net/web/creative/lincoln/speeches/gettysburg.htm. Accessed December 20, 2011.

Lincoln, Abraham. "Second Inaugural Address." http://www.bartleby.com/124/pres32.html. Accessed December 16, 2011.

Lind, Michael. *The Next American Nation.* New York: Free Press, 1995.

Lipset, Seymour Martin. *The First New Nation: The United States in Historical and Comparative Perspective.* New York: Norton, 1979.

Lipset, Seymour Martin, and Gary Marks. *It Didn't Happen Here: Why Socialism Failed in the United States.* New York: Norton, 2000.

Lipski, John M. *Latin American Spanish.* London: Longman, 1994.

Lomnitz, Claudio. *Death and the Idea of Mexico.* New York: Zone Books, 2005.

Lomnitz, Claudio. *Deep Mexico, Silent Mexico: An Anthropology of Nationalism.* Minneapolis: University of Minnesota Press, 2001.

Lomnitz, Claudio. "Final Reflections: What Was Mexico's Cultural Revolution?" In *The Eagle and the Virgin: National Identity, Utopia and Memory in Mexico, 1920–1940*, ed. Mary Kay Vaughan. 335–50. Durham: Duke University Press, 2006.

Longfellow, Henry Wadsworth, *Hiawatha, a poem.* Electronic Text Center, University of Virginia Library. http://etext.lib.virginia.edu/toc/modeng/public/LonHiaw.html. Accessed December 22, 2011.

López, Tonatiuh Guillén. "Federalism and the Reform of Political Power." In *Mexico's Democratic Challenges*, ed. Andrew Selee and Jacqueline Peschard. 187–202. Washington: Woodrow Wilson Center Press, 2010.

Luce, Henry. "The American Century." *Life Magazine*, February 17, 1941.

Maclennan, Hugh. "After 300 Years, Our Neurosis is Relevant." In *Canada: A Guide to the Peaceable Kingdom*, ed. William Kilbourn. 8–13. Toronto: Macmillan, 1970.

Maclennan, Hugh. *Two Solitudes.* Toronto: McClelland and Stewart, New Canadian Library, 2009.

Maclure, Jocelyn. *Quebec: The Challenge of Pluralism.* Montreal: McGill-Queen's University Press, 2003.

Macpherson, C.B. *The Political Theory of Possessive Individualism.* Oxford: Oxford University Press, 1962.

Madsen, Deborah. *American Exceptionalism.* Edinburgh: Edinburgh University Press, 1998.

Mainwaring, Scott, and Timothy Scully, eds. *Democratic Governance in Latin America.* Palo Alto: Stanford University Press, 2010.

Mainwaring, S., T. Scully, and Jorge Cullell. "Measuring Success in Democratic Governance." In Mainwaring and Scully, *Democratic Governance in Latin America*, 11–50.

Mann, Thomas. *Joseph and his Brothers*. Trans. H.T. Lowe-Porter. New York: Knopf, 1948.

Marentes, Luis A. *José Vasconcelos and the Writing of the Mexican Revolution*. New York: Twayne, 2000.

McCarthy, Cormac. *All the Pretty Horses*. New York: Knopf, 1992.

McCrum, Robert, et al. *The Story of English*. London: Faber and Faber, 1992.

McDonald, Marci. *The Armageddon Factor: The Rise of Christian Nationalism in Canada*. Toronto: Random House, 2010.

McElroy, John Harmon. *American Beliefs*. Chicago: Ivan Dee, 1999.

Mead, Walter Russell. *God and Gold: Britain, America and the Making of the Modern World*. New York: Knopf, 2007.

Melville, Herman. *White Jacket*. New York, 1850.

Mencken, H.L. *The American Language*, 4th ed., with new material by Raven I. McDavid Jr. New York: Knopf, 1963.

Merquior, José G. "The Other West: On the Historical Position of Latin America." *International Sociology* 6, no. 2 (June 1991): 149–64. http://dx.doi.org/10.1177/026858091006002002.

Meyer, Michael C., and William L. Sherman. *The Course of Mexican History*. 5th ed. Oxford: Oxford University Press, 1995.

Meyer, Michael, and William Beezley, eds. *The Oxford History of Mexico*. New York: Oxford University Press, 2000.

Micklethwait, John, and Adrian Wooldridge. *God is Back: How the Global Revival of Faith is Changing the World*. New York: Penguin, 2009.

Miljan, Lydia. Review of Bruce Muirhead, *Dancing around the Elephant*. *Canadian Journal of Political Science* 41, no. 1 (March 2008): 237–38.

Miller, Marilyn Grace. *Rise and Fall of the Cosmic Race: The Cult of Mestizaje in Latin America*. Austin: University of Texas Press, 2004.

Miller, Perry. *Errand into the Wilderness*. Cambridge, MA: Harvard University Press, 1956.

Millet, Lydia. "Arizona." In Weiland and Wilsey, *State by State*, 26–34.

Mills, C. Wright. *The Power Elite*. New York: Oxford University Press, 1956.

Mize, Ronald, and Alicia Swords. *Consuming Mexican Labor: From the Bracero Program to NAFTA*. Toronto: University of Toronto Press, 2011.

Morgan, Edmund. *Inventing the People*. New York: Norton, 1988.

Morris, Ian. *Why the West Rules—For Now: The Patterns of History and What They Reveal about the Future*. New York: Farrar, Straus and Giroux, 2010.

Moyers, Bill. "Welcome to the Plutocracy!" November 3, 2010. Truthout. http://archive.truthout.org/bill-moyers-money-fights-hard-and-it-fights-dirty64766. Accessed December 22, 2011.

Nadeau, Jean-Benoit, and Julie Barlow. *The Story of French*. Toronto: Knopf, 2006.

National Public Radio. "The Brothers Koch: Rich, Political and Playing to Win." August 26, 2010. http://www.npr.org/templates/story/story/php?storyID=129425186. Accessed May 20, 2011.

Niemeyer, E.V., Jr. *Revolution at Querétaro: The Mexican Constitutional Convention of 1916–1917*. Austin: University of Texas Press, 1974.

Mapleleafweb. 1911 Federal Election in Canada. http://www.mapleleafweb.com/voter-almanac/1911-federal-election-canada. Accessed May 15, 2011.

Nissenbaum, Stephen. "Inventing New England." In Wilson, *The New Regionalism*, 105–26.

Noll, Mark A. *A History of Christianity in the United States and Canada*. Grand Rapids: William Eerdmans Publishing, 1992.

Nora, Pierre. *Realms of Memory: Rethinking the French Past*. New York: Columbia University Press, 1996.

O'Gorman, Edmundo. *The Invention of America: An Inquiry into the Historical Nature of the New World and the Meaning of its History*. Bloomington: Indiana University Press, 1961.

O'Shaughnessy, Hugh. "Pope Acts Against Incest Priest's Group," *Independent*, August 8, 2010.

Odum, Howard, and Henry Moore, eds. *American Regionalism: A Cultural Historical Approach to National Integration*. New York: Henry Holt, 1938.

Orenstein, Peggy. "The Coast of Dystopia." *New York Times*, January 15, 2010. http://www.nytimes.com/2010/01/17/magazine/17fob-wwln-t.html. Accessed December 18, 2011.

Pacheco, José Emilio. *City of Memory and Other Poems*. Trans. David Lauer and Cynthia Steele. San Francisco: City Lights, 1997.

Pansters, Wil C. *Citizens of the Pyramid: Essays on Mexican Political Culture*. Amsterdam: Thela, 1997.

Paz, Octavio. *The Labyrinth of Solitude: Life and Thought in Mexico*. New York: Grove Press, 1961.

Paz, Octavio. *El ogro filantrópico*. Barcelona: Seix Barral, 1979.

Paz, Octavio. Nobel Prize Lecture, 1990. http://www.nobelprize.org/nobel_prizes/literature/laureates/1990/paz-lecture.html. Accessed December 22, 2011.

Paz, Octavio. *Itinerary: An Intellectual Journey*. New York: Harcourt, 1994.

Pedrero, Enrique. *La cuerda tenso: apuntes sobra la democracia en México, 1990–2005.* Mexico: Fondo de Cultura Económica, 2006.

Peterson, Paul E. "What is Good for General Motors." *Education Next* 9, no. 2 (Spring 2009). http://educationnext.org/what-is-good-for-general-motors/. Accessed December 19, 2011.

Peyrefitte, Alain. *Le mal français.* Paris: Plon, 1976.

Phillips, Kevin. *American Theocracy.* New York: Viking, 2006.

Pratt, E.J. *Selected Poems.* Toronto: University of Toronto Press, 2000.

Purdy, Jedediah. *A Tolerable Anarchy.* New York: Vintage, 2010.

Quirk, Tom, ed. *The Portable Mark Twain.* New York: Penguin, 2004.

Ramírez, Enrique Jackson. "Presentación." In *Federalismo y relaciones intergubernamentales,* ed. Mariano Palacios Alcocer. 5–7. Mexico City: Senado de la República, 2003.

Ramos, Samuel. *Profile of Man and Culture in Mexico.* Austin: University of Texas Press, 1962.

Ray, Arthur. *An Illustrated History of Canada's Native People.* Toronto: Key Porter, 2010.

Reading, Andrew. "Chiápas is Mexico: The Imperative of Political Reform," *World Policy Journal* Vol. X1:1 (1994): 11–25.

Reuters. "Majority of Americans distrust the government." April 19, 2010. http://www.reuters.com/article/2010/04/19/us-americans-government-poll-idUSTRE63I0FB20100419.

Reyes, Alfonso. *The Position of America and other Essays.* Freeport: Books for Libraries Press, 1971.

Riding, Alan. *Mexico: Inside the Volcano.* London: Tauris, 1987.

Robbins, Jeffrey W., and Neal Magee, eds. *The Sleeping Giant Has Awoken: The New Politics of Religion in America.* New York: Continuum, 2008.

Robinson, Sinclair, and Donald Smith. *Dictionary of Canadian French.* Toronto: Stoddart, 1990.

Rodriguez, Victoria. *Decentralization in Mexico: From Reforma Municipal to Solidaridad to Nuevo Federalismo.* Boulder: Westview, 1997.

Rohatyn, Felix. *Bold Endeavors: How Our Government Built America, and Why It Must Rebuild Now.* New York: Simon and Schuster, 2009.

Romero, Fernando. *Hyper-Border: The Contemporary US-Mexico Border and its Future.* New York: Princeton Architectural Press, 2008.

Rosanvallon, Pierre. *La légitimité démocratique.* Paris: Seuil, 2008.

Ross, John. *El Monstruo: Dread and Redemption in Mexico City.* New York: Nation Books, 2009.

Rossiter, Clinton. "The Relevance of Marxism." In *Failure of a Dream? Essays in the History of American Socialism*, ed. John Laslett and Seymour Martin Lipset. 362–88. Garden City: Anchor, 1974.

Sacks, Oliver. *Oaxaca Journal*. Washington: National Geographic, 2002.

Saez, Emmanuel, and Michael R. Veall. "The Evolution of High Incomes in Northern America: Lessons from Canadian Evidence." *American Economic Review* 95, no. 3 (June 2005): 831–49. http://dx.doi.org/10.1257/0002828054201404.

Sanchez, Jean-Pierre. "'El Dorado' and the Myth of the Golden Fleece." In Haase and Reinhold, *The Classical Tradition and the Americas*, 339–78.

Sanford, Charles. *The Quest for Paradise: Europe and the American Moral Imagination*. Urbana: University of Illinois Press, 1961.

Saul, John Ralston. *A Fair Country: Telling Truths about Canada*. Toronto: Penguin, 2009.

Schalmon, Arthur, ed. *Websterisms: A Collection of Words and Definitions Set Forth by the Founding Father of American English*. New York: Free Press, 2008.

Schmidt, Arthur. "Making It Real Compared to What? Reconceptualizing Mexican History since 1940." In *Fragments of a Golden Age: Politics and Mexican Culture since 1940*, ed. Gilbert Joseph, et al. 31–55. Durham: Duke University Press, 2001.

Schuck, Peter, and James Wilson, eds. *Understanding America: The Anatomy of an Exceptional Nation*. New York: Public Affairs, 2008.

Semo, Enrique. *The History of Capitalism in Mexico: Its Origins, 1521–1763*. Austin: University of Texas Press, 1993.

Semple, Neil. *The Lord's Dominion: The History of Canadian Methodism*. Montreal: McGill-Queen's University Press, 1996.

Seneca. *Tragedies, Medea*. Trans. Frank J. Miller. Loeb Classical Library. Cambridge, MA: Harvard University Press, 1917.

Shorris, Earl. *The Life and Times of Mexico*. New York: Norton, 2004.

Siegfried, André. *The Race Question in Canada*. Toronto: Carleton Library, 1966.

Silva, Guido Gómez de. *Diccionario Breve de Mexicanismos*. lst ed. Mexico: FCE, 2001.

Smith, Rogers. *Stories of Peoplehood*. Cambridge: Cambridge University Press, 2003. http://dx.doi.org/10.1017/CBO9780511490347.

Solares, Ignacio. *Yankee Invasion*. Minneapolis: Scarletta Press, 2009.

Sombart, Werner. *Why is There No Socialism in America?* London: Macmillan, 1976.

Stiles, T.J. *The First Tycoon: The Epic Life of Cornelius Vanderbilt*. New York: Knopf, 2009.

Stout, Robert Joe. *The Blood of the Serpent: Mexican Lives*. New York: Algora, 2003.

Tagle, Silvia Gomez. "Nuevas Formaciones Políticas en el Distrito Federal." In *La Geografía del Poder y las Elecciones in México*, ed. Silvia Gomez Tagle and Maria Eugenia Valdes. 39–94. Mexico: Plaza y Valdes, 2000.

Tannenbaum, Frank. *Peace by Revolution: Mexico after 1910*. New York: Columbia University Press, 1933.

Taylor, Charles. *A Secular Age*. Cambridge, MA: Harvard University Press, 2007.

Taylor, Graham D. *The Rise of Canadian Business*. Toronto: Oxford University Press, 2009.

Taylor, Norman W. "The French Canadian Industrial Entrepreneur and His Social Environment." In *French Canadian Society*, ed. Marcel Rioux and Yves Martin. 271–95. Toronto: McClelland and Stewart, 1964.

Thoreau, Henry David. "Walking." In Vare, *The American Idea*, 431–44.

Thoreau, Henry David. *Journal, Volume 4: 1851–52*. Ed. Leonard N. Neufeldt and Nancy Craig Simmon. Princeton: Princeton University Press, 1992.

Tocqueville, Alexis de. *Regards sur le Bas-Canada*. Montreal: TYPO, 2003.

Todd, Douglas, ed. *Cascadia: The Elusive Utopia*. Vancouver: Ronsdale Press, 2008.

Torre, Monica de la, and Michael Wiegers, eds. *Reversible Monuments: Contemporary Mexican Poetry*. Port Townsend, WA: Copper Canyon Press, 2002.

Tucker, Robert W., and David C. Hendrickson. *Empire of Liberty: The Statecraft of Thomas Jefferson*. New York: Oxford University Press, 1990.

Turner, Frederick Jackson. "The Significance of the Frontier in American History," 1893. http://www.learner.org/workshops/primarysources/corporations/docs/turner.html. Accessed December 22, 2011.

Turner, John Kenneth. *Barbarous Mexico*, 1910. Excerpted in Jurgen Buchenau, ed., *Mexico Otherwise: Modern Mexico in the Eyes of Foreign Observers*. Albuquerque: University of New Mexico Press, 2005.

Ulin, David, ed. *Writing Los Angeles: A Literary Anthology*. New York: Library of America, 2002.

United States Supreme Court, *New State Ice Co. vs. Liebmann*, 285 US 262 (1932).

Vallières, Pierre. *White Niggers of America*. Toronto: McClelland and Stewart, 1971.

Vare, Robert, ed. *The American Idea*. New York: Doubleday, 2007.

Varese, Stefano. *Witness to Sovereignty: Essays on the Indian Movement in Latin America*. Copenhagen: Danish Ministry for Foreign Affairs, International Work Group for Indigenous Affairs, 2006.

Vasconcelos, José. *The Cosmic Race*. Baltimore: Johns Hopkins University Press, 1997.

Vázquez, Josefina Zoraida, and Lorenzo Mayer. *México frente a Estados Unidos: 1776–2000*. Mexico: Fondo de Cultura Economica, 2001.

Veblen, Thorstein. *The Theory of the Leisure Class*. New York: Macmillan, 1912.

Velasco, José Luis. *Insurgency, Authoritarianism, and Drug Trafficking in Mexico's "Democratization."* New York: Routledge, 2005.

Villegas, Daniel Cosío. *American Extremes*. Austin: University of Texas Press, 1964.

Villegas, Daniel Cosío. "Mexico's Crisis." In *The Mexico Reader: History, Culture, Politics*, ed. Gilbert M. Joseph and Timothy J. Henderson. 470–81. Durham: Duke University Press, 2002.

Vulliamy, Ed. *Amexica: War along the Borderlines*. New York: Farrar, Straus and Giroux, 2010.

Wagner, Erica. *Gravity: Stories*. London: Granta, 1997.

Webster, Noah. "Dissertations." *Simplified Spelling Society Newsletter* (Spring 1986): 20, 21.

Weiland, Matt, and Sean Wilsey, eds. *State by State: A Panoramic Portrait of America*. New York: Harper and Collins, 2008.

Weintraub, Sidney. *Unequal Partners: The United States and Mexico*. Pittsburgh: University of Pittsburgh Press, 2010.

Whitehead, Lawrence. *Latin America: A New Interpretation*. London: Palgrave Macmillan, 2006.

Whitman, Walt. *Complete Poetry and Collected Prose*. New York: The Library of America, 1982.

Wilkinson, Richard, and Kate Pickett. *The Spirit Level: Why Equality is Better for Everyone*. London: Penguin, 2010.

Wilson, Charles Reagan, ed. *The New Regionalism*. Jackson: University Press of Mississippi, 1998.

Wilson, Charles Reagan. *Baptised in Blood: The Religion of the Lost Cause, 1865–1920*. Athens: University of Georgia Press, 2009.

Wise, S.F. "God's Peculiar Peoples." In *The Shield of Achilles*, ed. W.L. Morton. 38–61. Toronto: McClelland and Stewart, 1968.

Wolin, Sheldon. *Democracy Incorporated.* Princeton: Princeton University Press, 2008.

Young, Eric van. *The Other Rebellion: Popular Violence, Ideology, and the Mexican Struggle for Independence, 1810–1821.* Stanford: Stanford University Press, 2001.

Zamorano, Abel Perez. "Los problemas estructurales del campo mexicano." In *México, Visión Global,* ed. Miguel Godínez and Alberto Martínez. 179–212. Mexico: Porrua, 2006.

Zea, Leopoldo. "The Actual Functions of Philosophy in Latin America." In *Latin American Philosophy for the Twenty-First Century,* ed. Jorge Gracia and Elizabeth Millan-Zaibert. Amherst: Prometheus, 2004.

Zea, Leopoldo. *The Latin-American Mind.* Norman: University of Oklahoma Press, 1963.

Index